KARL MARX AND RELIGION

Also by Trevor Ling

The Significance of Satan (SPCK)
Buddhism and the Mythology of Evil (Allen and Unwin)
Buddha, Marx and God (Macmillan)
Prophetic Religion (Macmillan)
A History of Religion East and West (Macmillan)

Karl Marx and Religion

In Europe and India

Trevor Ling

First published in 1980 by
THE MACMILLAN PRESS LTD.
London and Basingstoke
Associated companies in Delhi Dublin
Hong Kong Johannesburg Lagos Melbourne
New York Singapore and Tokyo

Printed in Hong Kong

British Library Cataloguing in Publication Data

Ling, Trevor
  Karl Marx and religion.
  1. Religion and sociology
  2. Communism and religion
  3. Marx, Karl – Religion
  I. Title
  200'.92'4   BL60

ISBN 0–333–27683–3
ISBN 0–333–27684–1 Pbk

Contents

Preface

THERE are two substantial reasons why the study of religion should include some study of Marxism. One is that the work of Karl Marx has had an important bearing on methods of study in history and sociology, two of the major disciplines employed in the study of religion. The other is that Marxism, whether rightly or wrongly, has been regarded by a considerable number of scholars as a religion; those who have characterised it in this way have included historians, philosophers, theologians and sociologists. One has, therefore, to make some attempt to decide how far, if at all, this view can be justified.

This book is intended to serve as an introduction to these and other issues which arise when one juxtaposes the name of Karl Marx and the word 'religion'. The sources available to the student and general reader for the exploration of the area of interaction between these two are not very plentiful, however. There is the collection of extracts entitled *Marx and Engels on Religion* (1957). This contains most of the significant references to European religion (with the notable exception of Karl Marx's 'On the Jewish Question'). Beyond Europe, Marx's concern with religion was, understandably, very slight. He did, however, during the 1850s have occasion to concern himself with Indian religion, and the articles in which his references on this subject are to be found have been collected in *Marx – Engels on Colonialism* (1968). They are also to be found in S. Avineri's *Karl Marx on Colonialism and Modernisation* (1968). What is still needed at the introductory level is a study which will fill in the background details, provide historical connecting links between the various references to religion made by Marx from time to time, and set both the European and the Indian references within a comparative framework. The present volume will, it is hoped, help to meet this need. On the way a little time will be spent here and there in exploring some related issues such as Max Weber's sociology of religion in relation to that of Marx, especially with regard to India, and in considering the significance, in relation to Marx, of one or two other notable figures such as Jakob Boehme, William Blake and Sri Aurobindo Ghose.

Earlier versions of certain parts of this book have appeared in various journals, and acknowledgement is gratefully made of permission to use the material here in revised form. Chapter 3 originally appeared in *New*

Community (the Journal of the Community Relations Commission) vol. II, no. 2 (1973). Part of chapter 6 was published in *The University of Leeds Review*, vol. 16, no. 1 (May 1973), under the title 'Max Weber in India'. An earlier version of chapter 8 was delivered as one of a series of public lectures at the University of Lancaster. Part of chapter 9 was presented as a paper to the British Sociological Association Study Group on Religion at Durham in 1975 and appeared subsequently in *Religion*, vol. 5, Part 2 (Autumn 1975). In connection with the typing of the present work I gladly acknowledge the swift and efficient help given by Mrs Jeanne Lockett of the Department of Comparative Religion, University of Manchester.

November 1977   Trevor Ling

Abbreviations

MECW   *Karl Marx and Friedrich Engels, Collected Works*, (London: 1975), Lawrence and Wishart, continuing.

NYDT   *New York Daily Tribune.*

Part One

Marx and Western Religion

1 Marx's Critique of State Religion

AT the outset it may be appropriate to provide, for the benefit of the reader who is not a specialist in Marxist scholarship, a brief account of the major components of the Marxist-Communist tradition.

The word Marxism has been used in a variety of ways and within a number of different perspectives.[1] Historically there is, first of all, the early life and intellectual activity of Karl Marx himself. Second, in 1844 Marx, at the age of twenty-six, met a man who was to be from then on his lifelong friend and collaborator, Friedrich Engels; the classical system of German Marxism may be regarded as having its chronological starting point in the year of their meeting. Nevertheless the antecedent period, especially the years Marx spent at the University of Berlin and after that as a journalist, were of substantial, indeed, seminal importance in the development of classical German Marxism.

The next major development was the use of the writings of Marx and Engels by V. I. Lenin and other members of the Russian *intelligentsia*. With the adoption of their ideas as the basis of the newly established Soviet state in 1917, Soviet Marxism came into being. Its development, particularly in the Stalinist period, was of a kind which led some Marxists outside the Soviet Union to adopt positions highly critical of Soviet Marxism. This reaction is often now referred to as Neo-Marxism, and consists of a strong emphasis on the philosophical thought of Mark and Engels and a rejection of the contribution of Soviet Marxists, and, also by some, a rejection of what they regard as the Engelsian element in Marxism. There is a tendency, too, among some Neo-Marxists to concentrate on what they see as the humanism of the early Marx, as distinct from what may be called the cosmocentric view found in classical Marxism. Neo-Marxists in Europe include such writers as Erich Fromm, Lucien Goldmann and Herbert Marcuse. The border between Marxism-Leninism and Neo-Marxism is possibly the most appropriate location for Georg Lukács and Louis Althusser. Marcuse, in particular, is also a prominent representative of the more strongly socio-political (rather than philosophical and intellectual) emphasis found among the New Left.

Another way of setting out the various kinds of Marxism is to see them in terms of (a) a philosophical approach; (b) a sociological method of analysis; and (c) an ideology for political action. The philosophical approach relies heavily, although not entirely, on the early Marx, especially the now famous *Economic and Philosophic Manuscripts of 1844,* which were first published in German in 1932.[2] The 'great sociological or socio-historical theses worked out by Marx' as Maxime Rodinson has called them, can be regarded as 'solidly established and acceptable to all thinkers on the scientific plane'. As Rodinson trenchantly adds, 'this does not mean denying the ideological obstacles that have stood in the way of their general acceptance, and which still stand in their way. There were also ideological obstacles to acceptance of the law of how bodies fall.'[3] George Lichtheim, at the end of his study of Marxism, refers to the recent fertilisation of sociology, history, and anthropology by what (according to traditionalists) are unorthodox concepts, concepts that are clearly of Marxist origin.[4] It is as a politico-economic ideology and a programme for action that Marxism has most clearly split along numerous party and even national lines. Our concern in this chapter, however, is limited mainly to the first two aspects which have been described: as philosophical approach, and as sociological method, but will include also some suggestion of the way these provide the basis for a Marxian critique of some ideological and historical political developments.

(i) *Marx and religion*

Three stages in the development of Marx's attitude towards religion can be distinguished. The first was one of conventional acceptance, during his school days, of Christian ideas. The second was his outright rejection of Christian and all theistic beliefs on philosophical grounds, adopted during the time he spent as a student at the University of Berlin. The third was his critique of the use made of religion by the state, and the socio-economic analysis of the interests represented by the state which this prompted him to undertake; this third stage begins with his work as a journalist in 1842 and lasts for the rest of his life.

The first of these three stages has been described in detail by David McLellan, and the reader is referred to his excellent books dealing with this period.[5] The evidence from the schooldays consists mainly of three essays which Karl Marx wrote for his *Abitur* or school-leaving certificate. He attended the High School in the town of Trier, his birthplace, for five years until he was seventeen (1830–35). He studied Latin, Greek, French,

German, mathematics, history and religion. The three essays for his *Abitur* were on .a Latin theme: 'Does the Reign of Augustus Deserve to be Counted Among the Happier Periods of the Roman Empire?'; a religious theme: 'The Union of Believers with Christ According to John 15, 1-14, showing Its Basis and Essence, Its Absolute Necessity, and Its Effects'; and an essay on a subject of the writer's own choice, for which Marx chose to write on 'Reflections of a Young Man on the Choice of a Profession'.[6]

In the essay on religion Marx argued that the study of history, which he said was 'the great teacher of mankind', showed that human nature had from antiquity tried to raise itself to a higher level of morality, and that thus 'the history of mankind teaches us the necessity of union with Christ'. For, ' . . . when we consider the history of individuals, and the nature of man, we immediately see a spark of the divine in his breast, and enthusiasm for the good, a striving after knowledge, a desire for truth'.[7] These aspirations were vitiated, however, by human sin; but this could be overcome by the union of believers with Christ. Such union would afford a 'happiness which the Epicurean in his simple philosphy and the more profound thinker in the furthest depths of knowledge seek in vain'. Only the believer, bound to Christ and through him to God, could know such happiness, and this, he concluded, 'makes for a finer and more elevated life'.[8]

McLellan comments that while the essay seeks to show how Christianity was necessary for the full moral development of mankind, it nevertheless reveals a 'distant and colourless deistic conception of God'.[9] This may have reflected the attitude of his teacher, Joseph Küpper, the Protestant pastor of the parish and a man of strongly rationalist sentiments, and possibly also of his father, Heinrich; Jew by birth and the son of a rabbi, Heinrich had been received into the Lutheran church the year before Karl's birth (in order to conform to German legislation of 1816 which gave Jews the option between such conformity and life in a ghetto). Heinrich was virtually a humanist, 'who believed with Condorcet that man is by nature both good and rational'.[10] The High School at Trier was remarkable at that period for the views of its headmaster, Johann Hugo Wyttenbach, who 'educated his pupils in a free, cosmopolitan spirit, entirely dissimilar to that prevailing in the royal Prussian high schools', a spirit which showed itself in an absence of the conventional attitude towards the state religion; 'wearisome phrases about throne and altar, prevalent, nay prescribed at the time, were never used by him', records Nicolaievsky.[11] He notes also that on account of its reputation for 'indiscipline' and what were regarded by the local officials as some partially 'ill-disposed' members of its staff it was, during the years 1833–5 when Karl was there, 'the subject of dozens of official reports'.

Nevertheless it was here that the young Marx was exposed to the influence of French liberal ideas, especially those of Rousseau. These came out very clearly in the third of the essays for his *Abitur*, a German composition on the subject of choosing a career: 'If we choose the career in which we can do humanity the most good, burdens cannot overwhelm us, since they are nothing but sacrifice for the benefit of all. . . . Experience rates him as the happiest who has made the greatest number happy, and religion itself teaches us the ideal for which all strive, to sacrifice oneself for humanity.'[12] This, comments Nicolaievsky, remained 'the fundamental maxim of Marx's life' and notes that 'to work for humanity' is said to have been his favourite motto.

The second stage in the development of Marx's attitude towards religion began in 1836 when he moved from the University of Bonn, where he had spent a year after leaving High School, to go to the University of Berlin. The change of environment would have been fairly drastic. Trier, and to some extent Bonn, were old-world towns; Trier certainly was a relatively quiet country town, remote from the growing industrial development of the Ruhr and Rhineland cities. Berlin, on the other hand, already surrounded by industrial areas, was an 'immensely large and populous city, modern, ugly, pretentious and intensely serious'. It was the administrative centre of the Prussian state, and also provided the meeting place for radical intellectuals who were opposed to the state.[13]

The journey to Berlin in October 1836 took five days by mail coach; the railways, which were at that period beginning to be built, had not yet reached Trier.[14] At the University of Berlin Marx was admitted to the Faculty of Law, and registered for three courses in criminal law, Roman law, and anthropology. Almost from the beginning of his time in Berlin he began to feel strongly attracted towards philosophy, but he pressed on with his studies in law, so that by the end of the first semester he had worked through and evaluated texts and original sources well beyond what the curriculum required.[15] But the appeal of philosophy was still strong, particularly because of the influence of Hegel who had been professor of philosophy at Berlin until his death in 1831. This influence continued to be very strong, especially in the circle of his more radical disciples who were known as the Young Hegelians. When Karl Marx looked back over his first year in Berlin, in a letter to his father dated 10 November 1837, he wrote 'I had to study law, and above all felt the urge to wrestle with philosophy.' His reading of the legal and historical sources led him to try 'to elaborate a philosophy of law covering the whole field of law',[16] an attempt which, he adds, covered almost 300 pages. The effort began to affect his health; '. . . moreover I had neglected nature, art and the world, and shut the door on my friends'.[17] On medical advice he went away to the country, to Stralow, where, as he says, he matured 'from an anaemic weakling into a man of robust bodily strength'. What was more, through some friends he met while he was there, he came to know about a newly formed *Doktorklub* in Berlin. This was a group of university lecturers and high-school teachers who constituted an important element in the radical Young Hegelian movement; its members included the theology lecturer, Bruno Bauer, the history teacher, Karl Friedrich Köppen, and the geography teacher, Adolf Rutenberg.[18] They met in a small café or in private rooms and here, Marx says, 'many conflicting views were expressed, and I became ever more firmly bound to the modern world of philosophy from which I had thought to escape'.[19] He had already, during his holiday at Stralow, become more fully acquainted with Hegel's philosophy 'from beginning to end', and so strongly was he now preoccupied with it that, with the encouragement of his university teachers, he eventually wrote his doctoral dissertation on a philosophical theme, namely the 'Difference Between the Democritean and Epicurean Philosophy of Nature'.[20]

One of the principal characteristics of the Young Hegelians, and the *Doktorklub* especially, was the application of philosophy to contemporary religious and theological ideas. Bruno Bauer, who taught theology, engaged in unreserved criticism of the status of the canonical Gospels as historical accounts of the life of Jesus; in this he followed a lead originally given by David Strauss in his *Life of Jesus*, published in 1835. The argument which Strauss had advanced, that the Gospels portray not an historical Jesus, not a first-century Jew of Palestine, but rather a Hellenised Christian myth in the form of historical narrative, was at first resisted by Bruno Bauer when he was asked to review Strauss's book, but later he adopted an equally radical attitude himself. This was manifested in his critical studies of the Fourth Gospel and the Synoptic Gospels.[21] As a result the Prussian state authorities secured his dismissal from his post at Bonn University. The effect of this upon the Young Hegelians was an intensified concern with the question of the relation of religion and the state. It is worth noting that more recently, in the late 1970s, English theologians have still been trying to acquaint the body of lay believers with the accumulated results of the historical and literary criticism of the New Testament in a book entitled *The Myth of God Incarnate*, with a similar but now somewhat

muted and more impotent response from the ecclesiastical establishment.[22]

The criticism of accepted Christian dogmas, which became a strong
feature of the discussions in the *Doktorklub* in Berlin, had its effect on
Marx's thought, combined as it was with the influence of the work of
Ludwig Feuerbach which he was now reading. Feuerbach, born in 1804,
had studied Protestant theology at the University of Heidelberg. The
speculative approach of one of the theologians, Daub, had led Feuerbach to
attend Hegel's lectures in philosophy. Daub studied under Feuerbach for
two years and eventually gave up theology, and having gained his
doctorate he became a university lecturer and in 1830 published
anonymously, no doubt for reasons of discretion, a book on death and
immortality[23] in which he argued that the only possible kind of human
survival from death was not that of any individual 'soul' but that of the
'human spirit' as a whole. It was the human spirit, if any at all, rather than
any 'divine' spirit which was transcendent. The authorities discovered that
he was the book's author and he was dismissed from his post at the
University of Erlangen, but was later reinstated. He continued to write on
the same theme, criticising Christian theology from the standpoint of
philosophy. In particular he criticised Hegel's position as one of 'rational
mysticism'; Hegel had dissolved the distinction between God and man by
regarding man's life as a material projection of the ideal realm, the divine.
Feuerbach, while he agreed that there was no ontological distinction
between human and divine, argued that the relationship had been stated
upside down; he proposed to set the matter the right way up by insisting on
the reality of the natural world, of which the divine was a projection. These
ideas were fully developed in his book *The Essence of Christianity*,
published in 1841.[24] In this he argued that belief in God was the result of
Man's tendency to abstract the finest qualities found in human nature, to
project this artificially constructed perfection of being on to an ideal realm
beyond the human realm, and to call this 'God'. What are in reality human
qualities are thus made to appear as a divine power to which man aspires, to
which he is subject, and in whom alone he can find fulfilment. Man is
obsessed by religious imaginings because man is divided against himself, or
alienated from his own true being. Feuerbach, describing the 'fundamental
idea' of his book, wrote as follows: 'The objective essence of religion,
particularly the Christian religion, is nothing but the essence of human,
and particularly Christian feeling; the secret of theology therefore is
anthropology. . . .'[25] By 'anthropology' here is meant, of course, the
scientific study of man in a general sense.

The concept of alienation, or estrangement *(entfremdung)*, was particularly important in Bruno Bauer's thought, and it was he who was responsible for the expression 'self-alienation' which was much used by the Young Hegelians.[26] Marx was a close friend of Bauer's, and for them both the year 1842 was in some senses critical. In May of that year, as we have noted, Bauer was dismissed from the University of Bonn. Marx saw this as an indication that his own chances of being appointed to a university teaching post had also virtually disappeared. He had already, however, begun to be involved in a new journalistic enterprise of a radical kind, the *Rheinische Zeitung*, which took over from an older paper published in Cologne and under the new management of some of Marx's friends and collaborators had started publication on 1 January 1842. From the outset the new paper was faced with the problem presented by the censorship of the press in the Prussian state. Marx's first article for the *Rheinische Zeitung* dealt with the liberty of the press and the publication of the proceedings of the Rhenish Diet.

(ii) *Marx on religion and the state, 1842–3*

Marx had already made a deep impression on the group in Cologne – one of them, Moses Hess, writing to a friend described Marx as 'the only *real* philosopher now living'; ' . . . he is still a young man (he is at most twenty-four years old)', but 'he combines the most profound philosophical earnestness with the most biting wit. Think of Rousseau, Voltaire, Holbach, Lessing, Heine and Hegel fused into one – I say *fused*, not just lumped together – and you have Dr. Marx.'[27] Certainly the article Marx wrote on the liberty of the press greatly increased the already growing circulation of the *Rheinische Zeitung* and he was asked to write as many more articles as he could. Before long the paper was attacked by an older and larger rival, the *Kölnische Zeitung*. The grounds of the attack were that it was impermissible in a newspaper either 'to spread philosophical and religious views . . . or to combat them'.[28] The *Kölnische Zeitung* leader-writer went on to say that 'the new philosophical school has been allowed to make most disgraceful attacks on Christianity'.[29] The cause of this concern for Christianity was concern for the stability of the state. The author of the leading article declared that the history of the ancient states showed that 'the decline of their greatness and power coincided with the decline of their religious culture'.[30] The argument, thus, was that since religion is a bulwark of the state, to attack religion was to attack the state.

Marx, in the series of articles which he wrote in reply in the *Rheinische Zeitung*, challenged this interpretation which, in his view, attributed too much autonomous reality to religion. 'To arrive at the truth', he wrote, 'the author's assertion must be directly reversed; he has stood history on its head. . . . It was not the downfall of the old religions that caused the downfall of the ancient states, but the downfall of the ancient states that caused the downfall of the old religions.'[31] The *Kölnische Zeitung* leader had declared that 'the greatest results of scientific research have so far only served to confirm the truths of the Christian religion'. Marx commented that although Christianity was so assured of its safety in the modern world and would not decline, the police nevertheless 'must be on their guard to see that philosophising newspaper writers do not bring about such a decline. . . . Christianity is sure of its victory, but according to Hermes [the *Kölnische Zeitung* writer] it is not so sure of it as to spurn the aid of the police.'[32]

Marx then pointed out that the Prussian state was not in fact based on 'Christianity' in any sense that could be agreed on. For in the first place its citizens included both Protestants and Catholics and these were not agreed on what *was* Christian. 'Do not you Protestants believe that Catholics misinterpret Christianity? . . . Feuerbach and Strauss have been more reproached for regarding Catholic dogmas as Christian than for declaring that the dogmas of Christianity are not dogmas of reason.'[33] The Prussian state was *not* founded on Christianity it was clear, he argued, or it would be a 'religious state'.

> The truly religious state is the theocratic state; the head of such a state must be either the God of religion, Jehovah himself, as in the Jewish state, or God's representative, the Dalai Lama in Tibet. [But] where, as under Protestantism, there is no supreme head of the church, the rule of religion is nothing but the religion of rule, the cult of the government's will.[34]

Marx here reaches a vital point in his analysis of religion in the Germany of his day, a hinge upon which considerable issues turn. He saw from his own experience and that of his contemporaries that recently philosophy had by no means served to confirm the 'truths' of 'received' Christian religion, and that it was as much due to the protection of the state as to the survival value of its dogmas that the German version of Christianity survived in Prussia. One was then led to ask, therefore, what interests of the state were being served in its protection of its own variety of Christianity.

Indeed, this question was part of a deeper one: what and whose interests *were* represented by the state? Not those of the entire population, it was clear, but rather a special section of the population. Such an interpretation seemed to be upheld by the study of the law of property and theft which Marx now began to make. The occasion for this was provided by debates in the Rhine Province Assembly on the Law of Thefts of Wood. Traditionally the practice of the common people in gathering dead wood from the forests had not been challenged, but by the 1840s agrarian crises and hardships, linked with growing industrial demand for timber, brought about a critical situation in which five-sixths of all the prosecutions in Prussia dealt with timber thefts; these were, in fact, mostly for pilfering of fallen wood; this, as Marx wrote, brought about 'the conversion of a citizen into a thief'.[35] In this way Marx's attention was focused for the first time on the material interests of the common people in relation to the state. As he himself put it seventeen years later: 'In the year 1842–3, as editor of the *Rheinische Zeitung*, I first found myself in the embarrassing position of having to discuss what is known as material interests. Debates of the Rhine Province Assembly on the theft of wood and the division of landed property . . . caused me in the first instance to turn my attention to economic questions.'[36] Engels also recorded that he had heard from Marx that it was through concentrating on the law of thefts of wood that he was led from pure politics to economic relationships, and so to socialism.[37]

Another article written by Marx, in the autumn of 1843, indicates that the major thrust of his criticism of religion was against religious collectivities; in this case it was against Judaism. In 1843 Bruno Bauer had published a work on the Jewish Question,[38] in which he had argued that the demand of the Jews in Germany for emancipation in political terms was misdirected. They were asking for this from a Christian state in which they lived as second-class citizens. Rather than acknowledge the authority of this German Christian state to give or withhold emancipation (which was a tacit admission of the legitimate authority of such a state), they should join with those in Germany who were, on theological and philosophical grounds, seeking to uncover the falsity of religious claims, *Jewish and Christian*. The strength of the opposition between Christian and Jew, according to Bauer, was a *religious* opposition; expose the weakness of both Christian and Jewish theology and there will remain no ground upon which Christians can exercise their self-claimed superiority over Jews. Bauer was in effect calling upon Jews not only to accept contemporary philosophical attacks on Christianity but on Judaism also, and to renounce their Judaism just as fully as they would reject the claims of Christianity. All would then stand together simply as citizens.

Marx rejected this approach to Jewish-Christian relations. Instead he turned attention towards the social and economic forms with which both Christian *and* Jewish religions are associated. Emancipation in a *political* sense only would be a poor gain. Political emancipation by itself, argues Marx, falls far short of real human freedom. The political status of *citizen* is an illusory freedom; the real inequalities and impairments continue to coexist with citizen-status, and they are rooted in inequalities in *private* or civil life which the state upholds and protects. This is the level at which emancipation is needed: emancipation from the ability of one man to coerce another man, or a multitude of men, *economically*. Without emancipation from the state which exists to maintain these conditions of life it is futile to speak of freedom in any *human* sense. It is as human beings rather than as *citizens* merely sharing political equality that men, whether Jews or Christians, should seek freedom. By dealing with religious differences politically, so that such differences have no support in the political realm, men may think that they have sufficiently dealt with the dangerous aspect of religion. In this they are mistaken. For although religion may no longer be effective in the political realm once it has been abolished politically, it nevertheless continues to manifest its spirit in economic, or civil life.[39] Such is Marx's argument.

In particular, he continues, this is true of the Jews. For a while the Jew (in Germany) may have no practical *political power*, Marx observes he enjoys another power, the *power of money*. 'Although theoretically the former is superior to the latter, in actual fact politics has become the serf of financial power.'[40] Marx's argument in his article, 'On the Jewish Question' then develops into a long series of loosely connected aphorisms concerning Judaism, Christianity, private property and money. These require fairly full quotation in order to be appreciated properly:

> Judaism has held its own *alongside* Christianity, not only as religious criticism of Christianity, not only as the embodiment of doubt in the religious derivation of Christianity, but equally because the practical-Jewish spirit, Judaism, has maintained itself and even attained its highest development in Christian society. The Jew, who exists as a distinct member of civil society, is only a particular manifestation of the Judaism of civil society.
> Judaism continues to exist not in spite of history, but owing to history. The Jew is perpetually created by civil society from its own entrails.

What, in itself, was the basis of the Jewish religion? Practical need, egoism. . . ?

Money is the jealous god of Israel, in face of which no other god may exist. Money degrades all the gods of man – and turns them into commodities. Money is the universal self-established *value* of all things. It has therefore robbed the whole world – both the world of men and nature – of its specific value. Money is the estranged essence of man's work and man's existence, and this alien essence dominates him, and he worships it.

The god of the Jews has become secularised and has become the god of the world. The bill of exchange is the real god of the Jew. His god is only an illusory bill of exchange. . . .

The *chimerical* nationality of the Jew is the nationality of the merchant, of the man of money in general.

The groundless law of the Jew is only a religious caricature of groundless morality and right in general, of the purely *formal* rites with which the world of self-interest surrounds itself.

Here, too, man's supreme relation is the *legal* one, his relation to laws that are valid for him not only because they are laws of his own will and nature, but because they are the *dominant* laws and because departure from them is *avenged*.

Jewish Jesuitism, the same practical Jesuitism which Bauer discovers in the Talmud, is the relation of the world of self-interest to the laws governing that world, the chief art of which consists in the cunning circumvention of these laws . . . .

Judaism could not create a new world; it could only draw the new creations and conditions of the world into the sphere of its activity, because practical need, the rationale of which is self-interest, is passive and does not expand at will, but *finds* itself enlarged as a result of the continuous development of social conditions.

Judaism reaches its highest point with the perfection of civil society, but it is only in the *Christian* world that civil society attains perfection. Only under the dominance of Christianity, which makes *all* national, moral, and theoretical conditions *extrinsic* to man, could civil society separate itself completely from the life of the state, sever all the species-ties of man, put egoism and selfish need in the place of these species-ties, and dissolve the human world into a world of atomistic individuals who are inimically opposed to one another.

Christianity sprang from Judaism. It has merged again in Judaism.

From the outset, the Christian was the theorising Jew, the Jew is therefore the practical Christian, and the practical Christian has become a Jew again.

Christianity had only in semblance overcome real Judaism. It was too *noble-minded*, too spiritualistic to eliminate the crudity of practical need in any other way than by elevation to the skies.

Christianity is the sublime thought of Judaism, Judaism is the common practical application of Christianity, but this application could only become general after Christianity as a developed religion had completed *theoretically* the estrangement of man from himself and from nature.

Only then could Judaism achieve universal dominance and make alienated man and alienated nature into *alienable*, vendible objects subjected to the slavery of egoistic need and to trading.

Selling is the practical aspect of alienation.* Just as man, as long as he is in the grip of religion, is able to objectify his essential nature only by turning it into something *alien*, something fantastic, so under the domination of egoistic need he can be active practically, and produce objects in practice, only by putting his products, and his activity, under the domination of an alien being, and bestowing the significance of an alien entity – money – on them.

In its perfected practice, Christian egoism of heavenly bliss is necessarily transformed into the corporal egoism of the Jew, heavenly need is turned into worldly need, subjectivism into self-interest. We explain the tenacity of the Jew not by his religion, but, on the contrary, by the human basis of his religion – practical need, egoism   . . .

Once society has succeeded in abolishing the *empirical* essence of Judaism – huckstering and its preconditions – the Jew will have become *impossible*, because his consciousness no longer has an object, because the subjective basis of Judaism, practical need, has been humanised, and because the conflict between man's individual-sensuous existence and his species-existence has been abolished. The *social* emancipation of the Jew is the *emancipation of society from Judaism*.[41]

If the value of Marx's work for sociology generally is assessed on the basis of passages such as those quoted above, it has to be rated very low. It would perhaps be unfair to expect from Marx a sophisticated analysis in terms of role relationships, group interaction, kinship-structures, belief-sets, and the many varieties of human deprivation other than economic,

---

* In the German original *Veräusserung*, here rendered as 'selling', and *Entäusserung*, as 'alienation'.

for example, of the kind which would be expected as the minimal requirement in a modern study in the sociology of religion. Nor would it be appropriate to expect him to take account of demographic realities, since reliable data on these would have been virtually unobtainable at the time when he wrote. If his work has had important consequences in history and sociology, as it has, this is mainly because as a philosopher and perhaps as a proto-sociologist he perceived certain patterns of inter-relationship between material and mental realities which had until then been insufficiently taken into account in the explication of human history.

Marx had a mordant, journalistic style and decorated his pages with many a clever and satirical turn of phrase. The kind of writing of which examples have just been given is good vigorous pamphleteering, intended no doubt to stir the blood, but it has little to offer by way of useful sociological analysis. Such grand superficialities as 'Judaism' and 'Christianity', when used in this sort of context, have no correspondence with historical realities; they are labels attached to Marx's own artificial, ill-perceived constructs. Weber, half a century later, dealing with the same kind of material, namely the relation between economic activity and religious identity, had a much finer sensitivity to the important differences within the broad category 'Christianity'. Weber perceived that this was a heuristically useless concept, and that, instead, analysis had to be carried out much closer to the ground than is provided in Marx's grand, heaven-and-earth vision of things. Weber shows that it is necessary to identify socio-economic correspondences much more sharply, and even if Weber's analysis was not sharp enough, especially when he went outside Europe, his perception of the significant differences within Christian religion between Catholic, Lutheran, Calvinist, pietist etc., and, again, between the Calvinism of the sixteenth century and that of the seventeenth, makes his work infinitely more valuable as sociology than that of his proto-sociological predecessor, for whose ideas, nevertheless, Weber had considerable admiration.

Those who regard Marx's ideology in the same way that the faithful of any other creed regard the revelation vouchsafed to their prophet will resent any questioning of its infallibility. What sociological study requires, however, is not the heat of ideological fervour, which is not difficult to generate, but the energy which will sustain careful analysis of all the data.

(iii) *Marx on religion and the state after 1843*

'For Germany, the *criticism of religion* is in the main complete', wrote Marx in 1844, rather prematurely perhaps.[42] He was referring primarily to the philosophical critique of Christian ideas which had been carried out by scholars such as Strauss, Bauer, and Feuerbach. It was this critique of the tenets of received Christian theology which was, in his view, now complete. The assumption he appeared to be making was that for anyone who considered the matter dispassionately there was nothing more to be said. There were still plenty of avowed believers in the Christian's God, but such belief was no longer universal and no longer stood without serious and substantial intellectual challenge; '. . . as the most capable and consistent section of Protestant theologians has maintained, Christianity cannot be reconciled with reason', he observed.[43]

Christian ideas continued in existence, nevertheless. This in itself was a matter of no significance from Marx's point of view: the major thrust of his critique was directed against the *use* of Christian religion by the socially and economically exploitative Prussian state for its own ends, and by other similar Western capitalist states for the same purpose. Protestantism was a religion well suited, by its own nature, for such use by political rulers, for its ideas had a particularly close correspondence with the condition of men in a capitalist society, especially when Protestantism was understood in terms of Feuerbach's analysis.[44]

Where religious beliefs, often of a mystical kind, were used to *challenge* oppressive governments, Marx applauded. He refers, for example, to 'the divinely' inspired Jakob Boehme,[45] and Engels writes with sympathy of the heretics and mystics whose opposition to state religion continued, he says, 'throughout the Middle Ages'.[46]

The importance for Marx of the philosophical critique of Christian religious ideas was to show that they were disputable, and that therefore the state which tried to encourage the public acceptance of such disputable ideas as true, and to be accepted unquestionably by all its citizens, evidently must have sinister reasons for doing so, whether conscious of this or not. It was this underlying, socio-political condition which prompted the state to require religion to be reverenced that Marx saw as of greater importance: 'The criticism of religion is the premise of all criticisms', that is, all socio-political criticism of the kind Marx was about to embark on in his 'Critique of Hegel's Philosophy of the State' *(Rechtsphilosophie)*, to which these words were the introduction. It was the state, said Marx, which produced 'religion' of the kind he was criticising:

> This state, this society, produce religion, an *inverted-world-consciousness*, because they are an *inverted world*. Religion is the general

theory of that world, its encyclopaedic compendium, its logic in a popular form, its spiritualistic *point d'honneur*, its enthusiasm, its moral sanction, its solemn complement, its universal source of consolation and justification. It is the *fantastic realisation* of the human essence because the human essence has no true reality. The struggle against religion is therefore indirectly a fight against *the world* of which religion is the spiritual *aroma*.[47]

Marx's thought had already, by the time he wrote these words in Paris in 1844, led him to envisage the necessity for the overthrow of an oppressive and falsely constructed regime. The 'struggle against religion' was relatively unimportant. As Marx went on to say, '. . . to abolish religion as the *illusory* happiness of the people is to demand their *real* happiness. The demand to give up illusions about the existing state of affairs is the *demand to give up a state of affairs which needs illusions*. The criticism of religion is therefore in embryo the criticism of the vale of tears, the halo of which is religion.'[48]

Marx's attention now moved away from direct concern with religion to a concern with the social and economic realities which, as he saw it, underlay the existence of the state. As he himself wrote in 1844, 'the criticism of heaven turns into the criticism of the earth, the criticism of religion into the criticism of law, and the criticism of theology into the criticism of politics.'[49] From 1844 onwards it was the analysis of the material means of human subsistence, of state law and the political organisation of human society which engaged Marx's attention. Although in his subsequent works he made occasional intermittent references to religion, these became fewer as time went by and were in any case largely the elaboration or application of the basic ideas concerning religion which he had worked out by 1844.

Even so, there is in these basic ideas an important criticism of European institutional religion which still warrants serious attention. The criticism of religion in *philosophical* terms may (or may not) have become more sophisticated since the 1840s; the criticism of religion in terms of its involvement with political rule, while it has received a fair amount of attention recently, is still an important item on the agenda for the study of religion in its world setting. One special reason for its importance is that Marx's critique of religion was directed specifically against the Protestantism of the Prussian state, and therefore against other forms of European state Protestantism. Whether his view, that the major reason for religion's continuance in a modern society is its encouragement or use by the bureaucratic state for its own purposes, can be applied to other types of religion and other cultural situations is a question which the study of religion in its world setting is bound to raise.

NOTES

1. 'There are a score, a hundred, nay, a thousand varieties of Marxism', is the view of a French Marxist sociologist and Islamic scholar, Maxime Rodinson. See *Islam and Capitalism* (1974), p. xiii. Similarly Peter Worsley, in his presidential address to the British Sociological Association, named at least ten different kinds. See P. M. Worsley, 'The State of Theory and the Status of Theory', *Sociology*, VIII, no. 1 (1974), p. 3.

2. See Bibliography under Marx, Karl.

3. M. Rodinson (note 1), p. xvi.

4. G. Lichtheim, *Marxism*, p. 395.

5. David McLellan, *The Young Hegelians and Karl Marx* (1969); *Marx Before Marxism* (1970); *Karl Marx: Early Texts* (1972); *Karl Marx: His Life and Thought* (1973).

6. See *MECW*, I, 3–9 and 636–42.

7. David McLellan, *Marx before Marxism* (revised edn, 1972), p. 52. For another translation see *MECW*, I, 637.

8. McLellan, p. 53; *MECW*, I, 639.

9. McLellan, p. 53.

10. Isaiah Berlin, *Karl Marx: His Life and Environment* (3rd edn, 1963), p. 29.

11. Boris Nicolaievsky and Otto Maenchen-Helfen, *Karl Marx: Man and Fighter* (1976), pp. 13f.

12. Ibid., p. 14.

13. Berlin (1963), p. 34.

14. Heinrich Gemkow, *Karl Marx: A Biography* (1968), p. 23.

15. Ibid., p. 26f.

16. *MECW*, I, 11f.

17. Ibid., 18.

18. Ibid., 734.

19. Ibid., 19.

20. Ibid., 25–105.

21. B. Bauer, *Kritik des Johannes* (1840); *Kritik der Synoptiker* (1841–2).

22. The response from the conservatives is still largely what it was in the 1830s; as, for example, in the case of (J. Hick, ed.) *The Myth of God Incarnate* (1977); now, however, ecclesiastical power over university appointments is not what it was then, even though the intention may be the same; the

Moderator of the General Assembly of the Church of Scotland on 30 June 1977 called on the authors of *The Myth of God Incarnate* to resign their university appointments. (*The Times*, 1 July 1977.)

23. *Gedanken über Tod und Unsterblichkeit* (1830).

24. *Das Wesen des Christentums*; translated by George Eliot (1854) as *The Essence of Christianity*, with an introduction by Karl Barth (1957).

25. Quoted by D. McLellan, *The Young Hegelians and Karl Marx* (1969), p. 88.

26. McLellan (1969), p. 64.

27. Nicolaievsky, p. 52.

28. *MECW*, I, 185. See also *On Religion*, pp. 17ff.

29. Ibid., 186.

30. Ibid., 189.

31. Ibid.

32. Ibid., 191.

33. Ibid., 197.

34. Ibid., 199.

35. Ibid., 225.

36. Ibid., 744, note 88.

37. *MECW*, III, 175.

38. Bruno Bauer, *Die Judenfrage* (Braunschweig, 1843).

39. *MECW*, III, 146–55.

40. Ibid., 171.

41. Ibid., 171–4.

42. Ibid., 175.

43. 'We leave aside, too, the fact that, as the most capable and consistent section of Protestant theologians has maintained, Christianity cannot be reconciled with reason, because "secular" and "spiritual" reason contradict with each other, which Tertullian classically expressed by saying, *"verum est, quia absurdum est"*.' *Rheinische Zeitung*, no. 193 (12 July 1842) Supplement, quoted in *MECW*, I, 190.

44. See, for example, Trevor Ling, *Buddha, Marx and God* (1966), pp. 122ff.

45. *MECW*, I, 190.

46. F. Engels, 'The Peasant War in Germany' (1850); see *On Religion*, p. 88.

47. *MECW*, III, 175.

48. Ibid., 176.

49. Ibid.

2 Marx and Mysticism

(i) *'The divinely inspired Jakob Boehme'*

PHILOSOPHY had always been hostile to Christian theology, in Marx's view. In an article written in 1842 he commented on the fact 'that all the philosophies of the past without exception have been accused by the theologians of abandoning the Christian religion'.[1] That Christian theology does not stand upon grounds of reason, Marx observed, had been maintained by 'the most capable and consistent section of Protestant theologians'. But the majority of theologians had simply attacked and denounced philosophy for its hostility to orthodox ecclesiastical dogma. Such attacks had been made, Marx added, even upon the philosophies 'of the pious Malebranch and the divinely inspired Jakob Boehme'.[2]

Marx appears to have had a considerable regard for some of Boehme's ideas. In *The Holy Family* (1844) he and Engels cite with approval Boehme's notion of *Qual* in the course of a discussion of materialistic philosophies. 'Among the qualities inherent in *matter, motion* is the first and foremost, not only in the form of *mechanical* and *mathematical* motion, but chiefly in the form of an *impulse*, a *vital spirit*, a *tension* – or a *Qual*, to use a term of Jakob Boehme's – of matter.'[3] Engels later (in 1892) commented on the meaning of this term used by Boehme:

> *Qual* is a philosophical play upon words. Qual literally means torture, a pain which drives to action of some kind; at the same time the mystic Boehme puts into the German word something of the Latin *qualitas*; his *'qual'* was the activating principle arising from, and promoting in its turn, the spontaneous development of the thing, relation, or person subject to it, in contradistinction to a pain inflected from without.'[4]

It is interesting to notice that Engels refers to Boehme as 'the mystic', and that Marx had described Boehme as 'divinely inspired', while regarding him philosophically as a materialist. To what extent they were familiar with the life and thought of this seventeenth-century mystic (1575 – 1624) is not absolutely clear. In general Boehme was remembered with some respect in nineteenth-century Germany, and elsewhere in Europe, including Britain and America. Hegel referred to him as this 'powerful mind'.[5] It may have been that the story of Boehme's encounters with Gregory Richter, the clergyman (*Pastor Primarius*) in the Silesian town of Goerlitz where Boehme lived, can account for some of the affinity they felt for him. It was in the context of Marx's own clash with the Prussian state on the issue of his critical attitude to Protestantism that his 1842 articles in the *Rheinische Zeitung* were written, and it was in one of these that the first of his references to Boehme was made.

It has been said elsewhere that Jakob Boehme was a man who had not a creed but a religious experience to communicate, and that around him, therefore, gathered a circle of disciples, 'a secret lodge of initiates or cautious group of half-heretics.[6] Like other mystics before and after him, however, Boehme protested his own orthodoxy and his adherence to the church and sacraments.[7] It is nevertheless true also that the parish clergyman, Gregory Richter, was a rigidly orthodox Lutheran who bitterly and savagely persecuted Boehme on the grounds that he had written an heretical book (Boehme's *Aurora*). The first outburst of this persecution occurred in the year 1612, and one has to remember that only twelve years earlier Giordano Bruno had been burned in Rome, and that Kepler and Galileo were still having none too easy a time with the ecclesiastical authorities. The Thirty Years War, which began in 1618, showed the depths of the passions of fear and hatred which could in that century be associated with theological and religious disputes. The second bout of persecution organised by Richter was in 1624, when he not only denounced Boehme from the pulpit but also incited mobs to attack his house. Richter published a broadsheet accusing Boehme of being a blasphemer, one who had denied God's infinity, and who arrogantly and presumptuously claimed knowledge he did not possess.[8]

But Boehme was not a man without wisdom, whether worldly or otherwise. He had a number of highly learned friends, and his mystical experience and writings have to be set against the background of his knowledge of contemporary science and philosophy. Martensen, his Danish biographer, refers to him as a 'highly enlightened layman, the great prodigy in the spiritual and intellectual world, the unexplained psychological enigma'.[9] Boehme was familiar with the astronomy of his day, as he himself records in *Aurora*: 'I have read the writings of the high masters . . . and have taken notice how they describe the course of the sun and stars, neither do I despise it, but hold that . . . good and right.' Nevertheless a mathematical account of the universe was, he considered, inadequate: '. . . they will have so much to learn that many will not comprehend the ground . . . all the days of their lives.' They stand upon the right ground, he affirms, but they need the teacher whom he has learned to follow: 'total nature'. He severely distrusted the capacity of reason alone.[10]

His idea that the entire universe had proceeded from a *Qual* was, as we have noted, what particularly attracted Marx and Engels. This has been explained as 'Boehme's word for reality's dynamic centre'. Qual is 'incomprehensible and irrational', the nature of every individual thing.[11] Ultimately Boehme sees a tension in the universe, between the absolutely good, the divine within God, and the unyieldingness of evil, a tension which must find discharge, an opposition which must find reconciliation. He was totally opposed to the predestinarian views of the Calvinists, and would have none of their eternal separation of the human world into the elect and the damned.

These, perhaps, are the two reasons which led Marx and Engels to mention Jakob Boehme in the favourable way they did: the unorthodox and apparently materialistic tenor of his religious ideas; and his conflict with ecclesiastical authority. It is difficult, however, to be quite sure that greater familiarity with his writings would not have diminished their regard for him somewhat, or that a fuller knowledge of the circumstances surrounding the publication of his works and of the aristocratic patronage he enjoyed would not have led them to see him as an ally of an élite class who were prepared to encourage certain kinds of religious ideas for their social and political value. Besides the German nobleman who promoted the publication of Boehme's works, one of the avowed admirers of his ideas was King Charles I of England.[12]

It is possible that Marx and Engels held a view of Boehme which still persists today in some quarters, that of the poor cobbler and visionary mystic who challenged the accepted religious forms and ideas of the Lutheran church, a view which is not consistent with the facts.[13] Some of Boehme's works have been acclaimed by those who live on the fringe of Christianity, especially the more theosophically inclined, as wise and deep alternatives to Christian orthodoxy, drawn from the springs of a rare visionary experience. Such a view can be taken more easily on the basis of certain selected works, for example *The Signature of All Things*, written at a time when Boehme had been engaged in a flirtation with the traditional and ancient lore of alchemy, but which he subsequently abandoned for more specifically theological writing. Boehme belongs firmly within the tradition of Christianity and passionately adhered, until his death, to its classical forms and institutions. On the other hand it is true that his exposition of the subject matter of the book of Genesis,[14] in which he expounded his theory of *Qual* which Marx and Engels applauded, was certainly unorthodox by the standards of his own day and still is by the standards of biblical fundamentalism. But he is not among the more socially radical of European mystics. It was this radical aspect of mysticism which chiefly attracted Marx and Engels. We noted earlier that Engels, writing of the Peasant War in Germany, referred to a revolutionary opposition to feudalism which 'took the shape of mysticism'. And, he adds, 'as for mysticism, it is well known how much sixteenth-century reformers depended on it. Münzer himself was largely indebted to it.'[15]

Mysticism, however, is a word to be handled with care. It can more easily confuse discussion than clarify it. We shall see later that there are non-European types of mysticism which can lend themselves to use by the state for political purposes just as easily as did the ecclesiastical Protestantism of Marx's Germany.

(ii) *The mysticism of William Blake*

Had Marx been looking for an example of a mystic who was a prophet and a rebel, a rebel in particular against the orthodoxy of state religion and the use of religion by authority for social control, he could have found one in William Blake, who died when Marx was nine years old.

Northrop Frye has commented that formerly 'allusions to Blake often used to assume that he was a timeless mystic who was dazed all his life at having been born in a definite place at a definite time; that he influenced no-one and that no-one influenced him; that his interests were occult and esoteric, with few parallels west of India.' He adds that this notion has now given place to a figure who is much more credible as having his origins very firmly in lower-middle-class, eighteenth-century, Nonconformist England.[16] This is not meant to deny that Blake was a mystic, but to point out what *sort* of mystic he was. Elsewhere Northrop Frye places Blake in the company of the Hebrew prophets.[17] For the prophet is 'the man who lives now in the true world which is man's home, and tries to make that world visible to others',[18] and certainly there is much of this in Blake's 'prophecies'. In Blake's own words, 'Man's perceptions are not bounded by organs of perception; he perceives more than sense (tho' ever so acute) can discover.' This faculty he refers to elsewhere as 'the Poetic or Prophetic character'.[19] Demonstration of truth on the basis of sense perception alone Blake calls 'Worldly Wisdom'. A culture entirely dominated by such worldly wisdom 'is hardly calculated to produce visionaries, saints, or revolutionists'.[20]

Politically, as J. Bronowski put it, 'Blake was a rebel in the plainest way. He supported the American and French Revolutions, he praised Washington and Lafayette, he wrote against George III and the King of France, and he was among the revolutionary friends of Tom Paine and Henry Fuseli and their publisher Joseph Johnson.'[21] Christ was, for Blake, a figure who contrasted with the jealous, fearful God of the Old Testament; he was the perpetually young figure, 'Christ with the sword; overthrowing the established orders and bringing danger and liberty in his two hands'.[22] Blake was the poet of the human spirit for he believed 'that the human was the divine – that man's divinity was wholly according to the measure of his humanity'.[23] One assessment of Blake's genius is in terms of striking paradox: he was a mystic who hated mystery, a Christian who really believed in Jesus, a man of such spiritual insight as to be worthy of being called both 'inspired' and 'prophetic'.[24] In short, Blake, with his sympathy for such rebels as the Ranters and Diggers, with his curses upon Church and State, and his prophetic utterances against imperialism, is one in whom radicalism is linked with religious fervour, and, as Bronowski sums it up, '. . . unless we can see as one the revolutionary idealism in Blake's politics and the Gnostic heresy in his religion, we simply do not see Blake.'[25]

(iii) From mysticism to monopolistic religion

All this stands in deep contrast to the exclusive and monopolistic spirit associated with a state religion. Unlike ecclesiastical dogmatism the way of the mystic does not lend itself easily to adoption as a state religion. For the mystic continually places the emphasis upon present experience, not upon ancient codification; on the reality he knows, not upon elaborate credal formulae embalmed in conciliar statements which all too clearly reveal the hundreds of hands that have worked them over and over until all life has been squeezed from the words. For this reason the mysticism of poet and prophet is unlikely to prove sympathetic to state religion, which relies heavily on the principle of *external* control and regimentation. The two are poles apart. In fact this is the view of their relationship which Arthur Koestler once suggested, in a series of contrasts which it will be useful to recall here.

In 1942, four years after he had left the Communist Party, Arthur

Koestler published a collection of essays entitled *The Yogi and the Commissar*. In the first essay Koestler suggested that all the possible attitudes to life could be arranged in the form of a spectrum. 'On one end of the spectrum, obviously on the infra-red end, we would see the Commissar.' The Commissar represents those who believe in what Koestler calls, 'Change from Without', that is, those who believe that the cure for all human ills is to be found in a reorganisation of the material basis of human life, particularly the means of material production and distribution, and who believe that the carrying through of this reorganisation justifies any methods and any kinds of behaviour towards those who get in the way. At the other end of Koestler's spectrum was 'the Yogi, melting away in the ultra-violet'. For him 'nothing can be improved by exterior organisation and everything by the individual effort from within'. Between these two extremes Koestler saw 'in a continuous sequence the spectral lines of the more sedate human attitudes.' On the whole, however, he found the central part of the spectrum fairly woolly; what he saw most clearly was the contrast between the two ends of the spectrum: '. . . the real issue remains between the Yogi and the Commissar, between the fundamental conception of Change from Without and Change from Within'.[27]

There is no evidence in the essay that, having become disenchanted with Communism, Koestler was looking with interest towards the other end of the spectrum. That the yogi had some kind of perverse fascination for him may perhaps be inferred from a book he wrote some years later, *The Lotus and the Robot*, which was, he says, a kind of sequel to his essay 'The Yogi and the Commissar'. But it is very clear from the later book that when it came to a choice, he felt extremely little *rapport* with the mystics he met in the course of his brief travels in India, and that he was not sorry to shake the dust of India off his feet.

Nevertheless, in 1942, it had seemed to him, as to a number of other intellectuals in Europe and America succumbing to the temptation to generalise about the human condition at a time when totalitarian ideologies were at the height of their power and repulsiveness, that the yogi was the most obvious symbol of the attitude to life which is diametrically opposite to that of the totalitarian regimes.

The yogi, for many of the disillusioned among that generation of intellectuals, was the embodiment of what they believed to be the lofty, detached, pure spirituality of India, unsullied by involvement with mundane or political concerns. It was a spirituality which they saw in sharp contrast to the crude materialism of the West. This was a viewpoint which Indian idealist philosophers who wrote in English, mainly for Western readers, had been spreading abroad for some time. However the great majority of the Indian educated classes, supported by masses of their fellow-countrymen, were at that time engaged in a very real, earthly struggle to overthrow British political power in India and achieve Indian (and Pakistani) national independence.

In his essay Koestler did not develop his concept of a spectrum of human attitudes, but left the idea in the fairly rudimentary stage at which it had come to him. It was sufficient for Koestler that at the other end of the spectrum, in total contrast to the yogi, was the commissar. But it is possible to connect these two extremes by means of a continuum of intervening types of religious organisation.[28] The spectrum is one which passes through the following stages: next to the yogi is the individualistic type of religion which has been described by Thomas Luckmann as 'Invisible Religion' and by Robert Towler as 'Common Religion'.[29] Next to this, and slightly more individualistic than the sect, comes the 'cult' type;[30] then the sect, less ephemeral and somewhat more persistent as a group formation than the cult. At the farther end the sect becomes an 'established sect'. The sect, however, in its primitive or its established form is certainly more individualistic, particularly in its notion of salvation, than the church-type which lies next to it on the spectrum. First comes the denominational church, such as the churches of the Baptists and Methodists, and then the national or state church, such as the Church of England. Beyond the state church, but similar to it in many ways, is the type we may call 'national religion', notable examples of which can be found in the Islamic world, in Pakistan and Malaysia for instance. Finally the transition is made from Islam, as a national and international religion, to Communism.

in sociological terms, is not difficult to show. The close similarity between them has been demonstrated in detail by Jules Monnerot in his *Sociology of Communism*. The nature of these parallels will be considered in our final chapter, in connection with the question: Is Marxism a religion? It is important to notice at this point that Koestler did not characterise his contrasting positions as religious; he called them 'human attitudes to life'. However, all the intervening gradations between the two, it has been suggested, are types of *religious* formation. Whether the easy transition from Islam to Communism means that the latter also is a religious formation, or whether at this point we pass from religious to non-religious, is a matter which must be left until various other matters have been considered.

What has to be noted at this stage is that so far as *Marx* is concerned there does *not* appear to be a necessary and absolute polarity between his attitude to religion and the attitude towards religion adopted by some mystics. This may be due to the fact that there is a range of types among mystics also. There were, apparently, some mystics with whom Marx felt some kind of *rapport*, as well as others with whom he had none; such *rapport* was very much a matter of their attitudes to official, orthodox religion, especially state religion. The point might be made that Koestler's contrast was between Communism and the *yogi*, that is the characteristically *Indian* type of mystic; we therefore need to know whether Marx was likely to have any kind of *rapport* with the Indian type. But to say there is only one type of Indian mystic would be to attribute an excessive importance to geographical differences. It would be to assume that the yogic type of mystic is *only* to be found in India, and that it is the only type to be found there.

The facts seem to be otherwise: no one, single continent or culture has prior claim to be regarded as the native place of mysticism, or even as the exclusive home of any one type of mysticism. Nevertheless the tendency to think of India as the characteristic geographical and cultural location *par excellence* for mystical religion, and to think of the Western hemisphere as characteristically un-mystical persists.

(iv) *The suppression of mysticism in Europe*

Rather than assume that India, *qua* India, has some special environmental, ethnic or social predisposition to produce a mystical type of religion, it would probably be more pertinent to examine the historical factors which in the West led to the suppression of the mystical attitude in religion. It would also be useful to enquire how (and when) the notion arose that Indian religion is predominantly 'spiritual' or 'mystical'.

While the West has, on the whole, since the beginning of the modern period, evaluated political and governmental achievement more highly than the exploration of a world behind the apparently real world of the physical senses, and has ascribed greater prestige to the control of political power than to the exploration of the nature of human consciousness and the purposes of human life, the mystical way is not entirely alien to the European religious tradition by any means. It is certainly to be found there, and has in the past had its notable exemplars and exponents. But it has more often than not been suppressed by the ecclesiastical – political organisation whose power it challenges. For mystical religion makes priesthood and the whole apparatus of monopoly-controlled sacraments as a means to salvation unnecessary. It is therefore seen as a threat to their priestly organisation by those who have a vested interest in the maintenance of ecclesiastical power as a means of social control. In the furtherance of this vested interest apparently objective theological and philosophical arguments can be produced in order to discredit mystical religion, and these have often proved very persuasive. Such arguments can be made to seem very sound, especially to those who are already predisposed by their own commitment, or by their official position as priests or dignitaries, to believe them. The Waldenses, the Beguines, the Beghards and many other similar groups of dissenters in late medieval Europe who rejected the necessity for sacerdotal institutions and emphasised the importance of the mystical way were all alike regarded as heretics and were suppressed by the ecclesiastical authorities. For the latter recognised the threat to the Church's material interests which such men represented. In France, England and Germany individual mystics, such as Amaury, Dinant and Eckhart, were condemned as blasphemers.[31] In Europe opposition to mysticism may have been given a superficial respectability in the eyes of some, by being buttressed with theological argument, but it is difficult to escape the conclusion that ultimately this opposition came from a concern to preserve at all costs the uniqueness of some monopolistic method of salvation, usually either that of the one 'true' Church or the one 'true' Book. To those who opposed mysticism it was axiomatic that the really crucial control of human affairs in this world was operated at the centres of *political* power; often this was through the agency of physical force, or the threat of it. At the end of the medieval period the competing, warring nation-states of modern Europe began to give full expression to this European-Christian veneration of politico-physical power. The assumption underlying a great deal of European historical writing is quite clearly that the ultimately decisive question is: who exercises political control? Those who chose to take an alternative view both of their own contemporary situation and of the history of Europe, a view which sees the really decisive element elsewhere and not in the political arena primarily, and who affirmed so, were, until recently, dismissed as eccentrics; to make doubly sure they were also persecuted as public enemies.

We can now return to the question of Marx's attitude to mysticism, and the extent to which this differed, if at all, from his attitude to state-established religions. It will be convenient to do so by reverting to Koestler's contrast between the two types, the yogi and the commissar. It should now be clear that the notion that these contrasting types can be identified as *cultural* types, Asian and Western respectively, is misconceived. Nevertheless the misconception persists, and from time to time receives reaffirmation either directly or indirectly. In its crudest form it can be set out as follows, in terms of contrasting stereotypes:

YOGI	COMMISSAR
Mystical	Practical
Spiritual	Material
Indian	Western
Religious	Anti-religious

This set of contrasts can be shown to be false. In the first place, as we have noted, the mystical type is not exclusively Indian; it can equally well be Western, as Marx recognised. In the second place, 'mystical' is of wider connotation than the Indian yogic type. In Western culture the mystic may be of the radical, prophetic type (such as William Blake); or he may be the follower of a codified form of mysticism, one which corresponds in its 'received' nature with the yogic type in that it consists in the following of a 'way'. In the third place, the commissar type is not exclusively Western. It is certainly not un-Indian necessarily. Sanskritic Brāhmanical culture is by itself no guarantee of spirituality, or of incompatibility with the attitudes of the commissar.

Finally, it would be entirely too crude to identify the yogi with a *religious* attitude to life, and the commissar, therefore, with an *anti-religious* attitude or even necessarily a Marxist attitude. If the distinction between what is Marxist and what is Communist – and particularly Soviet Communist – is borne in mind, it will be recognised, in the light of Marx's references to Boehme, *first*, that Marx himself was not so strongly opposed to mysticism, especially to the radical-prophetic mystic, as he was to state Protestantism; and *second*, that Marxism is not simply identifiable with the attitude of the commissar, whether Soviet or of some other kind. Whatever those who declare themselves followers of Marx may find it legitimate to do in his name, Marx himself was strongly critical of the exercise of state power in support of an ideology, whether or not this was conventionally 'religious'. This, however, is a point to be discussed more fully in the final chapter. Meanwhile we may note that Marx was not only opposed to the use of the power of the state in the interests of ideology, but having experienced its effects in Prussia was also convinced of its futility and knew its counter-productive effect.

Marx's criticism of religion was directed against the Protestantism of the

Prussian state in the early part of the nineteenth century. Yet it has been assumed by some Marxists that this critique applies automatically to any other system of belief and conduct which goes by the name of 'religion'. The assumption made by such Marxists is that all systems known as 'religions' share with nineteenth-century German Protestantism those features of the latter which were criticised by Marx. This is a vast assumption, and one which can only be made confidently by those who are unaware of the many important differences which exist within the broad, undefinable, and simplistically conceived category 'religions'.

It is essential, therefore, if extrapolation from German Protestantism to other systems of belief and conduct is to be made at all, to start from a reiteration of the distinctive points of Marx's critique. Protestantism was for Marx, first, a set of beliefs in an unreal world: '. . . the religious world is but the reflex of the real world.' Second, in asserting this, Marx was reversing the order of things as it was expounded in Protestant doctrine, namely, that this present world is but the reflex of the real world, the spiritual or heavenly world, which is man's true home. He accused the Prussian state bureaucracy of fostering Christian doctrine and of protecting it against profane attack because the members of that bureaucracy recognised the value of such theological ideas as a means of justifying the economic inequalities of their contemporary society. The Prussian state was, as Marx saw it, a committee to defend the interests of the property-owning élite. Whether or not this view was justified does not affect the issue that this is the essence of Marx's critique of religion; this is where, in his view, religion was disreputable.

Such a critique, formulated within German society, can therefore properly be applied to other religious ideologies and institutions only where these reveal the same kind of characteristics. For in India also, for example, it is maintained that the true nature of man is revealed only in some supramundane realm which is normally unknown to mortals, a realm to which they can have no access except by means of a special kind of initiation not naturally available to men and not discoverable by the unaided human intellect, and which therefore has to be vouchsafed to them by those who alone possess supernatural authority, that is by priests of some kind. Wherever *such* a doctrine is maintained and promoted by those who find it a useful and convenient means of deflecting the attention of economically dispossessed classes of society, and especially where priests do so to a significant degree through the agency of the state, whether in Europe or in India or elsewhere, *there* the Marxist critique of religion is appropriate. Wherever religion is not of this disposition, the Marxist critique may be inappropriate.

It is important to notice, for example, that the conditions outlined above are not present in the case of the mystical religion of the sort which was mentioned earlier in connection with William Blake. If there is a form of mysticism to which Marx's critique of religion applies, it must firstly be one which bases itself on the claim that mystical insight is the monopoly possession of a spiritual élite who alone can give initiation and guidance to the neophyte, and secondly one in which such claims are used as a means of social control. In other words 'mysticism', like religion, is a single term which refers to a plurality of distinguishable phenomena. Of the major varieties of mysticism two have been indicated here; one is the orthodox or codified mysticism which is entrenched in a monopolistic system of spiritual hierarchy; the other is that which springs from the spontaneous experience of a man who may, if he is known at all to the world at large, appear as poet or prophet, and who is more likely than not to be a critic of the spiritual élitism associated with the first type, especially if it exists in an institutionalised form in close alliance with the state, as in the case of the official Buddhism of Thailand.[32]

If the foregoing is accepted it becomes possible to consider how far Marx's critique of religion applies to the various examples of religion outside Europe. A full investigation would be a large and long undertaking. Here we shall be limited to the attempt to provide examples of how the investigation might proceed; the cases to be considered are first that of England, and second that of Brāhmanical religion in India.

Political convenience has played a large part in shaping the public religious life of England in past centuries. Insistence on conformity to orthodox belief and practice because it was in the political interest of England's rulers was a prominent factor in giving the Church of England its particularly compromising character. There are, therefore, two reasons for including an account of the Anglican attempt to monopolise the religious life of England which lasted from the late seventeenth century to at least the beginning of the twentieth. The first is that England in this respect provides a close parallel to the religious situation which existed in Prussia in Marx's youth, and therefore an indication that Marx's critique of religion was by no means eccentric. The second is that, with this attempted Anglican dominance of English religion in mind, we shall more easily be able to understand how the English who went to India in the eighteenth and nineteenth centuries were predisposed to the idea that every land (including India) would have its own dominant religion which it might be politic to preserve for reasons of social control.

NOTES

1. *MECW*, vol. I, p. 190.

2. Ibid.

3. Ibid., vol. IV, p. 128.

4. The quotation is from *Socialism, Utopian and Scientific*, see *MECW*, vol. IV, p. 691.

5. Hans L. Martensen, *Jacob Boehme 1575-1624: His Life and Teaching* (trs. by T. Rhys Evans, 1885), p. 3.

6. John Joseph Stoudt, *Sunrise to Eternity: A Study in Jacob Boehme's Life and Thought* (1957), p. 176.

7. Ibid., p. 183.

8. Ibid., pp. 177f.

9. Martensen, p. vii.

10. Stoudt, pp. 93f.

11. Ibid., p. 25f; see Boehme, *Vierzig Fragen von der Seele*, vol. i, pp. 51f and *Erklärung über das Erste Buch mosis*, vol. VIII, p. 20 and vol. XXIX, p. 9.

12. Martensen, p. 3.

13. That there would not be much justification for such unfamiliarity with Boehme's life and work is indicated by the number of studies on the subject published in Germany in the middle decades of the nineteenth century, of which the following are examples: Jules Hamberger, *Die Lehre des deutschen Philosophen Jakob Böehme* (München, 1844); Hermann Adolph Fechner, *Jakob Böehme: Sein Leben und Seine Schriften* (Goerlitz, 1857 [a prize essay]); Albert Peip, *Jakob Böehme: Der Deutsche Philosoph* (Leipzig, 1860); G. C. Adolf von Harlech, *Jakob Böehme und die Alchemisten* (Berlin, 1870).

14. See note 11.

15. K. Marx and F. Engels, *On Religion* (Moscow, 1957), p. 88.

16. Northrop Frye (ed.), Blake: *A Collection of Critical Essays* (1966), p. 4; see also Max Plowman, *Blake's Poems and Prophecies* (1927), p. viii.

17. Frye, p. 25.

18. Ibid., p. 26.

19. Ibid., p. 145.

20. Ibid., p. 146.

21. *William Blake: A Selection of Poems and Letters*, edited with an Introduction by J. Bronowski (1958), p. 9.

22. Ibid., p. 12.

23. Plowman, *Blake's Poems*, p. xiv.

24. Ibid., p. xxi.

25. J. Bronowski, *William Blake and the Age of Revolution* (1972), p. 15.

26. The following five paragraphs originally appeared in an article by the present writer entitled 'The Yogi and the Commissar Revisited' in *Bulletin of the John Rylands University Library of Manchester*, vol. 57 (Spring 1975), no. 2., pp. 388f.

27. A. Koestler, *The Yogi and the Commissar* (1965), p. 15f.

28. For an expansion of the description of this spectrum see the article cited in note 26.

29. Thomas Luckmann, *The Invisible Religion* (1967), and R. Towler, *Homo Religiosus* (1974), ch. 8.

30. See David A. Martin, *Pacificism* (1965), p. 194.

31. See Trevor Ling, *A History of Religion East and West* (1968), p. 280.

32. On this see, for example, Samboon Suksamran, *Political Buddhism in South-East Asia* (1977); and Trevor Ling, *Buddhism, Imperialism and War: Burma and Thailand in Modern History* (George Allen and Unwin: London, 1979), chs. 5 and 6.

3 State Religion in England

THAT the Church of England represents the major religious affiliation of the people of England today appears at first sight undeniable. But *how* major is this majority? What degree and kind of majority does the Church of England possess in relation to all other religious bodies or communities now present in this country? These are important questions which receive too little attention in contemporary discussions on such matters as religion and the state, religious education in state schools and so on. A little thought, plus a little historical research, soon reveals the fact that to be established as 'top religion' requires more than numerical superiority. It is essential also to be the major body in terms of *power*, political, social and economic – as well as in terms of numbers of adherents – and on this count the Church of England certainly has a clear lead over all other recognised kinds of religious affiliation in England. Its lead in terms of numbers is not nearly so overwhelming, however, in spite of the common assumption that the Church of England is *the* form of religion of the English people, and that therefore on *that* score it has a right to some sort of presidential position in religious affairs. Its lead, and its presiding role, is in terms of its power. The reasons for this lie in the political history of modern England, and need to be clearly understood if any attempt is to be made to look objectively at the situation of religious pluralism which obtains in this country today.

(i) *Citizens and Anglicans – facts and fictions*

It is little more than 300 years since the attempt was made in this country to bring the entire population within one comprehensive religious–political institution, the Anglican Church. The Act of Uniformity of 1662 was the giving of legal status to the notion that the terms 'citizen' and 'Anglican' were synonymous. Even though 'citizen' and 'churchman' may have been synonymous in the medieval period, they were not in the seventeenth century. Yet the idea was given a currency which still persists in certain quarters. The phrase 'religious minority' is often assumed to mean, if not actually 'non-Anglican', at least in these days when Nonconformists are conforming more and more, then a 'non-British Council of Churches type of religious body'.

This is at a time when all religious bodies, Anglican included, are in fact minorities within a predominantly non-church English society, even if one uses such favourable criteria of real membership (in the Anglican situation) as the numbers attending Easter communion. The largest single component in the religiously pluralistic situation in England today, as in many other Western countries, is the unaffiliated, non-ecclesiastical majority. This majority is not necessarily religionless, as Luckman and others have pointed out.[1] Moreover such a majority, managing to live independently of active membership of any ecclesiastical body, has existed in England for some centuries. It seems fairly certain that it existed in the seventeenth century, and that the Act of Uniformity gave official standing to a fiction that has been maintained by upholders of the Anglican establishment ever since. In the seventeenth century the form of it was that – apart from those small minorities, both Protestant and Catholic, which refused to conform – there existed a religious solidarity within English life and that its name was the Church of England.

Certainly in 1662 it was illegal to be absent from Anglican worship. Non-attendance 'could entail the forfeiture of two-thirds of a man's estate'.[2] Those most likely to suffer such loss of property were the Catholic landed gentry. 'But Protestants who would not go to church might forfeit all their goods and be required on pain of death to promise, under oath, to leave the realm for ever.'[3] These penalties were not widely enforced after 1660, however; the main intention from that time was to exclude non-Anglicans from positions of influence in the state. This was in order to neutralise what was felt to be the continuing political danger to the state represented by the presence of Puritans and Papists, and in order to establish strong government with the aid of a politically reliable church. For it was still possible for religious beliefs and organisations to be used to justify revolt. Penalties on non-conformist religious belief and affiliation were therefore proportionate to the political danger they represented. Thus the idea was allowed to gain currency that, in England, all those who are not actively Nonconformist are *de jure* 'Church of England', whether or not they actually fulfil their ritual obligations.

(ii) *Early ecclesiastical and non-ecclesiastical systems*

In the seventeenth century, however, the *fact* was that England was a religiously plural society. It is outside the purpose of this chapter to seek evidence of religious pluralism in England in earlier centuries, although, in the writer's view, the idea of a religiously undifferentiated medieval society owes more to ecclesiastical theory than to historical research and analysis. As Keith Thomas has recently written: 'Not enough justice has been done to the volume of apathy, heterodoxy, and agnosticism which existed long before the onset of industrialism. . . . What is clear is that the hold of organised religion upon the people was never so complete as to leave no room for rival systems of belief.'[4] So far as the sixteenth and seventeenth centuries are concerned, Thomas's book indicates just how copious is the evidence of heterodox systems of belief and practice among the majority of the people. Of a more refined sort was the atheism and scepticism of such men as Christopher Marlowe, Sir Walter Raleigh, and many other Elizabethan intellectuals.[5] In addition to this aristocratic distaste for Christian tenets, there was not only the much greater volume of popular scepticism and heresies which would lead to the rejection of formal religion[6] but, even more significantly, there was positive adherence to other, clearly non-Anglican cults and practices. These Thomas classifies under three headings, magic, astrology, and witchcraft. There was a strong interconnection between magical and astrological beliefs, and between these and witchcraft; the whole formed a composite popular paganism which appears very similar to that which can be found today, in some Asian countries for example, where there are large areas of society still at the pre-industrial stage. Such popular pagan systems of belief and practice have as their purpose the relief and cure of the many forms of human suffering which cannot be effectively dealt with in any other way in a pre-scientific and pre-industrial society. And such suffering, caused by disease, famine, ignorance, and natural calamities, was very great in seventeenth-century England.

Certainly 'the contemporary clergy saw the cunning folk and astrologers as their deadly rivals . . . because they resented a competing pastoral agency, and because they were anxious to replace a magical explanation of misfortune by a theological one'.[7] In some countries in Asia the official priesthood or clergy, such as Brāhmans or Buddhist monks, have traditionally maintained an open frontier with such popular paganism, gradually infusing it with religious values and providing men with means of intellectual transition from paganism to a more sophisticated world-view. Catholicism has often established the same kind of relationship. But in seventeenth-century England this was precluded by the nature of Anglicanism. So magical beliefs came to compete with Anglicanism, in the sense that the two had become reciprocally exclusive systems, and that magic, like official religion, claimed to deal with the ills arising out of the changes and chances of this fleeting life by calling upon supernatural powers. Both magic and astrology appear to have undergone a boom in England after the Reformation and before the full effects of the Industrial Revolution were felt.[8]

As opposed to the fictional state of affairs legalised in the Act of Uniformity, the real religious situation in England in the seventeenth and the first half of the eighteenth centuries was that large numbers of the ordinary people adhered to an interconnected system of supernatural beliefs and practices which may be called popular paganism. The term paganism is wholly appropriate to a situation in which at least 80 per cent of the population lived in the countryside, and experienced the human sufferings and misfortunes of a rural, pre-industrial society.[9] In addition there was the Anglican church, its clergy and regular attenders; and there were those who, unlike the mass of the people, were sufficiently positive in their theological or ecclesiastical views to declare their non-conformity; these were of two main kinds, Catholic and Protestant. The former consisted of the surviving Catholic aristocracy with their dependants and workpeople and were concentrated in certain areas of England, especially the northern and western counties. The latter consisted of Baptists, Independents (later called Congregationalists) and Presbyterians. Their areas of strength were the eastern counties which lay to the north of the Thames, and the south-west.[10]

In terms of religious culture, pre-industrial England can be seen as consisting of two main types fairly evenly divided, with non-ecclesiastical popular pagan culture on the one hand and ecclesiastical on the other, consisting of the Anglican, Nonconformist and Catholic churches.

(iii) *The Act of Uniformity and differing non-conformisms*

The practical consequence of the Act of Uniformity had been to re-emphasise the division between Anglican and non-conformists (both Protestant and Catholic). These divisions themselves were not new, of course. The hostile attitude of Puritans towards the Church of England during the interregnum between the death of Charles I and the Restoration of the Monarchy in 1660, was itself a powerful cause of the corresponding hostility shown by Anglicans towards Puritans after 1660. This time, however, the Anglicans were not subsequently displaced from power, and those Puritans who now emerged under the name of

Protestant Dissenters came to form a subordinate, continuing element in the cultural life of England.

It is important to identify this subordinate culture accurately. The Anglican party's decision, effected in the 1662 Act, was to reject the principle of a religiously plural nation in favour of uniformity. But since religious pluralism already existed, the consequence was the polarisation of the distinctively ecclesiastic bodies between conformist and non-conformist. Since that time, therefore, all religious minorities in England, apart from the Anglicans, have been non-conformist: this applies whether they were Catholic, Jewish, Muslim, Hindu, Pentecostalist or any other. But among all these differeng kinds of non-conformity it is possible to distinguish two main types: (1) Protestant Dissenters and, later, the secular dissenters; and (2) Catholics, Jews and various Asian minorities. The former type may be seen as *contra-cultures*; whereas the second are basically *sub-cultures*.[11] Between the two types there was little affinity or co-operation, except that in certain respects the sub-cultures have been the beneficiaries of the achievement of the contra-cultures in resisting the monopoly claims of the Church of England.

If Anglicanism became, after 1660, 'distinctively the upper-class religion',[12] Protestant non-conformity consisted largely of men and women 'who prided themselves on their independence'. They were more numerous in towns and cities than in the countryside; some were artisans, others were merchants. Inevitably they developed a social solidarity, if only in reaction to the avowed attempts of high-church Anglicans to destroy them altogether. The culture which developed among them was a contra-culture; it arose in contradistinction from and hostility to the upper-class Anglican culture of the gentlemen of England and their dutiful, rustic dependants, gentlemen who are exemplified in Addison's Sir Roger de Coverley. Barred from universities and schools, Nonconformists organised their own academies, from which eventually came the ministers of the Nonconformist congregations, supported financially by the contributions of the local congregation. This was one reason why such congregations were more easily maintained in towns and cities, where it was easier to gather a number of members sufficiently large to support a minister economically. These two cultures developed and persisted, side by side, as 'church' and 'chapel' almost to the end of the Victorian period, and continued to correspond with divisions in party politics, social ethics, and economic roles.[13]

The Catholic non-conformists were also subject to civil discrimination and disabilities, until the Catholic Emancipation Act of 1829. Even though the social position of the Catholic landowners gave them some immunity from the contempt which the Anglican upper classes showed towards Protestant Dissenters, they remained politically suspect, as well as religiously obnoxious, to many Anglicans. The Catholic community, more often than not, was an extension of the aristocratic or landowning Catholic family, under the leadership of the nobleman who supported the priest and provided the chapel for the celebration of Catholic sacraments. A map showing the distribution of the Catholic county families in eighteenth-century England would be, observes Gay, 'a good distribution map of Catholicism'.[14] Rather than developing as a contra-culture, Catholicism continued within the English environment until the early nineteenth century as a distinct sub-culture, having some affinities with cultures outside England.

Another example of this kind was the Jewish community. Expelled three and a half centuries earlier, under Edward I, Jews again began to settle in England in the seventeenth century. But this was at first a mere trickle, the settlement of a few hundred, until the year 1690 when Ashkenazi Jews began to arrive in greater numbers; this necessitated the founding of three new synagogues in London between that year and 1761. The attitude of Protestant Dissenters towards the Jewish community in England during this period may well have been as ambiguous as that of Oliver Cromwell. On the one hand he is credited with having welcomed their re-entry during the period of the Protectorate, out of sympathy with a religiously persecuted minority and especially because his Puritanism, with its strong emphasis on the Old Testament, would have given him an affinity with this people of the Book. On the other hand he is said to have been opposed to extending religious toleration to those 'who deny the divinity of our Saviour',[15] and to have agreed to the admission of Jews largely because of the economic benefits which would accrue to England, and thereby be denied to the Low Countries, through the diverting into London of refugee Jewish merchants and bankers from Spain. None the less the Protestant Dissenters of the eighteenth century, upholders of the principle that no man should suffer public discrimination on the purely personal matter of his religious belief and practice, would have been to that extent allies of the Jews who were now inhabiting the city of London, where Protestant Dissenters also had one of their strongholds of resistance to Anglican conformism. Certainly, by the beginning of the nineteenth century, the London assembly known as the Protestant Dissenting Deputies were giving such help as they could to the Jews, according to Bernard Manning, who writes: 'In 1831 they petitioned both Houses to repeal laws attaching any civil disqualifications to Jews, asking especially for an amendment to this declaration. They remarked that they, having themselves been recently relieved from such disabilities, felt most anxious that no class of their fellow-citizens should so suffer.'[16] They had earlier, Manning claims, been ardent supporters of the movement for Catholic Emancipation.[17]

(iv) *Erosion of Anglicanism in the nineteenth century*

The religious situation in England, and in particular the pattern of adherence to the various ecclesiastical bodies, Anglican and non-Anglican, had considerably altered by the middle of the nineteenth century. The major fact in the change which had occurred was the large extent of secularisation of the working people. Briefly, what had happened was the erosion of popular paganism under the gradually growing influence of scientific ideas and, more particularly, technological invention, the mechanisation of workshops, and the increase in the number of industrial towns and cities. Magical and astrological beliefs and practices certainly did not die out entirely,[18] but many aspects of their appeal were gradually eroded as it became possible for human misfortune to be alleviated in other than magical ways. A second important fact to be taken into account in the one hundred years preceding 1850 was the growth of Methodism. Both factors, the spread of secularism and the growth of Methodism, affected the relative strength of the religious establishment *vis-à-vis* the total population.[19]

The growth of secularism among the non-worshipping majority during the period of the Industrial Revolution also has the marks of a contra-culture. It has an affinity with the Protestant dissenting contra-culture, in that it too was a rejection of Anglican conformity arising from within the native population. One of the effects of the Act of Toleration had been that some of those who formerly had attended church unwillingly now did so no longer: once dissenters' worship was tolerated, they had the alibi of being able to claim, even though spuriously, that they were absent from church because they were dissenters. As the Bishop of Norwich wrote in 1692: '. . . A liberty now being granted, more lay hold of it to separate from all manner of worship to perfect irreligion than goes to them' (sc. to the dissenting places of worship).[20] This rejection of Anglicanism by those who had been bound to it simply by the nature of their circumstances was thus added to the religious absenteeism that already existed, as we have seen, among those sections of the population which adhered only to popular paganism for solace and spiritual comfort.

The extent of the erosion of Anglicanism was revealed in the Census of 1851, and shocked the Anglican hierarchy into attempts at reorganisation. In 1840 it had been estimated generally that the percentage of non-churchgoers among the urban working class varied, from place to place, between 75 and 90 per cent.[21] In 1821 the number of seats in Anglican churches in Sheffield totalled 4000, of which less than 300 were rent-free, that is, available for the working class. The population of Sheffield at this time was 16 times the total number of seats – 65,275. This means that only about 6 per cent of the total population of Sheffield could have attended Anglican services, even had all the churches been full. The evidence is that they were not and that 3 per cent is a liberal estimate for the Anglican population of Sheffield at that time. The 'numerous lower classes' who would thus not have been able to gain admission to Anglican worship even had they wished to were regarded by John Henry Newman as 'the new Goths and Vandals to destroy civilisation'.[22] At the end of the nineteenth century Winnington Ingram, the Bishop of Stepney, reported a census of church attendance taken by a working man in his factory of 2000 workers. Only 5 of these 2000 had ever been to church; 3 were Catholics, 1 was a Dissenter, and 1 an Anglican. Ingram commented that the 'immense majority of working men go neither to church nor chapel'. He added with candour: 'It is not that the Church has lost the great towns; it has never had them.'[23]

(v) *Rural Anglicans, urban Catholics, Jews and others*

Thus it was not in urban England, particularly in the great cities, that the numerical strength of Anglicanism was to be found; if anywhere it was in the countryside. This is roughly the situation today when, as Gay observes, it has 'most influence in the remoter, isolated areas such as Herefordshire'.[24] On the other hand it was in the towns and cities that non-Anglican religious bodies had their greatest numerical strength. Even in 1780 'nearly 40 per cent of the Catholics in England were to be found in London'.[25] After the inflow of Irish immigrants, in the wake of the potato famine of the late 1840s, the number of Irish-born in the population of England was 3 per cent. As almost all of these were Catholics, and as this percentage has to be increased by the addition of English-born Catholics, it is clear that the Catholic percentage was probably over 3 per cent. Most of these Catholics were living in towns and cities: '. . . London, Liverpool, Manchester, Leeds, Bradford, Sheffield, Newcastle and Birmingham. It was the Irish immigrants who made Roman Catholicism an urban phenomenon.'[26]

During the 1880s and 1890s the Jewish population of England increased rapidly. This was due to the continuous influx of refugees from persecution in Russia. Some settled in London. Others, landing at the east-coast port of Hull with the intention of crossing the country to Liverpool, there to re-embark for America, settled instead *en route* in the cities of the West Riding and of Lancashire, notably Leeds and Manchester. Jews also formed themselves into urban communities. This was necessitated partly by the requirements of Jewish religious culture, such as the need for a synagogue which could best be supported by a concentration of Jewish population, schools for the education of children, Jewish burial grounds, and Jewish slaughter-houses for the provision of ritually acceptable meat. It was partly, also, a consequence of the fact that the work which Jews could undertake, and in which they soon came to be prominent, such as the clothing industry, was usually of an urban rather than a rural kind. Four per cent of the total population of Leeds is Jewish and this is in fact the highest percentage; in terms of absolute numbers there are larger concentrations in the cities of Manchester and London.

Adherence to Anglicanism is generally lower in urban areas than it is in rural ones. In the countryside, where a traditional way of life and social structure survive longer than in the cities, Anglicanism is more at home and better represented in terms of the percentage of the population who avail themselves of its rites and ceremonies. In the urban context, that is, in areas where the culture of modern industrial society is more prominent, Anglicanism is weaker in percentage terms. In all of the 12[27] most densely populated dioceses of the Anglican Church, the number of Easter communicants in 1962 was less than 4 per cent of the total population of those areas.[28] In the 4 most densely populated industrial areas (London, Manchester, Liverpool and Birmingham), the numbers were less than 3 per cent. In the same areas, the corresponding Catholic figures in 1962 were 6.9, 10.9, 13.8 and 6.5 per cent.[29] These large, densely populated areas also contain the highest concentrations of other non-Anglican religious denominations or communities – Protestant non-conformists, Jews and more recently arrived Muslim, Hindu and Sikh communities from the Commonwealth.

(vi) *Anglican power; religious minorities; secular majority*

If in the characteristic centres of urban industrial society and culture non-Anglicans outnumber Anglicans, it has also to be remembered that *all* these religious communities, Anglican and non-Anglican alike, are minorities within a predominantly secularised majority, that is, among those who are virtually without any active religious affiliations. It is clear, therefore, that in modern England Anglicanism is the 'major' religious community only in the sense that it possesses major power, especially political and social. This inheritance of political power has been carefully guarded and, when it was possible to do so, has been used in order to check any growth in the rights or status of other bodies. As late as 1847, for example, a parliamentary Bill for the removal of civil and religious disabilities affecting Jewish citizens met with strong opposition from Anglican clerics; it was opposed in the House of Lords on the grounds that its effect would be to 'de-Christianize the legislature and imperil the country's religion', and was rejected by 163 votes to 125.[30]

It might be argued that the Church of England has now declined in power so far that it is no longer in a position to affect the rights or the freedom of the other religious minorities in this country. Although in terms of numbers of worshippers it has lost the advantage it once may have had over these other bodies, nevertheless, 'considered socially, it is formidable', as Leslie Paul remarks.[31] But the same writer also observes that in general 'the massive shift of the Church from the centre to the periphery of affairs simply, and perhaps properly, reflects the shift which has taken place in the faith of ordinary men and women'.[32] In other words, *vis-à-vis* the institutional religious life of this country, the Church of England succeeds in retaining a dominant position, not because it is the most prominent or progressive or relevant religious organisation in the industrial society of modern England, but for other reasons.

One of these, perhaps the major one, is the monopolist claim which was implicit in the Act of Uniformity, and the continuance of this claim by the Church of England during the succeeding centuries, and the fact that the Church is, by law, established. It is possible to see also some reasons why the claim tends to be accepted by the general public in England. The Anglican clergy are more numerous than other clergy;[33] probably more numerous than Catholic priests and Free Church ministers combined. This, together with the special position of bishops in political life, gives them a major presence. Another reason is that the judgement that the Church of England is the major religious body in this country is made by commentators who are themselves mainly middle-class, and in whose milieu it still retains 'major' status, much more than it does among the working-class population. Such commentators are usually representatives of an influential professional class whose adherence to Anglicanism is of a cultural and social kind, and which does not necessarily take the form of church attendance.

So far as the national life as a whole is concerned, the predominant element is what may be called secular. A better word might be 'profane', in its original sense of 'outside the temple' or not belonging to a sacred community. Certainly that is the major common characteristic of this now predominant class – the unchurched. This does not mean, however, that they have no interest in religion. Young people in this unchurched class will often be found to be those who have consciously rejected some conventional, institutional form of religion, but who have a strong interest in religious issues and in finding a satisfactory religious view of life. Not a few are attracted by Eastern religion, usually in its more mystical forms – Yoga, Zen, Sufism, and so on. For every one of the fairly small number of English members of local Buddhist and other societies, there are many more who have taken a serious interest in the ideas and the way of life represented by these non-Western faiths. The contribution which such religious concerns make to the emerging 'alternative culture' or, in the terms used in this paper, —*contra-culture*' among young people needs to be taken into account; it is a rich area for systematic research.

So, alongside the Asian communities in this country, alongside what exist at present fairly recognisably as Asian religious *sub-cultures* – mainly Hindu, Muslim, and Sikh – is this potentially sympathetic element in the new contra-culture.

It has thus become clear that in numerical terms the established church is now among the minority religious communities, and it also clear that the secular or 'profane' majority is not necessarily irreligious, but includes religious and non-religious elements within its total non-ecclesiastical spread. Thus the time would seem to have come for a reappraisal of the whole situation, and certainly a very much more precise use of terminology whenever there is talk of 'religious minorities' or 'minority religions'. Discrimination in religious matters is not unknown – witness the denial of the use of redundant churches to 'other religions' whose adherents wish to purchase them and make use of them for religious purposes.[34]

NOTES

1. Thomas Luckmann, *The Invisible Religion*; see also, e.g. 'Common Religion' by Robert Towler and Audrey Chamberlain, in *A Sociological Yearbook of Religion in Britain: 6*, ed. by Michael Hill (1973). Luckman's term 'invisible religion', and Towler's and Chamberlain's 'common religion' refer to the religious beliefs of the common people as they are beginning to be uncovered in the course of sociological research, as distinct from the kind of pattern of beliefs which it is supposed that the majority of people in a traditionally Christian country hold. See also what is said later in the text concerning 'popular paganism' in seventeenth-century England.

2. J. R. Western, *Monarchy and Revolution* (1972), p. 158.

3. Ibid.

4. Keith Thomas, *Religion and the Decline of Magic* (1971), p. 173.

5. For details see Thomas, p. 167.

6. Ibid., p. 169ff.

7. Ibid., p. 637.

8. Ibid., p. 639.

9. In 1801 only 11 per cent of the nation lived in places of over 100,000 population.

10. See John D. Gay, *The Geography of Religion in England* (1971).

11. The terms are used here in the senses suggested by J. Milton Yinger, in his paper 'Contraculture and Subculture', *American Sociological Review*, vol. 25, no. 5 (Oct. 1960), pp. 625–35. A *contra-culture* exists where there is a strong element of conflict between a sub-society and the whole society, and where many of the norms and values held by the former 'are specifically contradictions of the values of the dominant culture' (p. 629). A sub-culture, on the other hand, 'is not tied in this way into the larger cultural complex'; sub-culture norms are derived from some other culture than that of the major society within which the sub-culture exists; they 'are not, to any significant degree a product of (the) interaction' with the larger culture. In the case of Catholics in England it is primarily the large majority, the Irish immigrants, who are referred to here as a sub-culture. In the case of the minority of 'old Catholics', their cultural norms were derived originally from aristocratic and pre-industrial England. It is significant that, in the nineteenth century, hostility to Irish Catholic immigrants and to East-European Jewish immigrants was expressed more usually in *cultural* rather than religious terms, certainly among the working class. The same is true where an attitude of hostility towards Asian immigrants occurs today; it is usually cultural differences, such as

language, food-habits, dress, social and personal customs, community and solidarity, rather than religious differences, which are the cause of alienation. It is among the formally religious minority of Englishmen that the religious differences receive attention.

12. G. M. Trevelyan, *English Social History* (3rd edn, 1946), p. 253.

13. See George Clark, *The Later Stuarts: 1660–1714* (2nd edn, 1956), p. 24; and Peter Mathias, *The First Industrial Nation* (1969), p. 11.

14. Gay, p. 86.

15. Cecil Roth, *A History of the Jews in England* (3rd edn, 1964), p. 157.

16. Bernard Lord Manning, *The Protestant Dissenting Deputies* (1952), p. 211.

17. Ibid., p. 203ff.

18. As Keith Thomas points out, p. 668.

19. The rapid growth in the number of adherents to Methodism in the first hundred years of the movement's history added considerably to the non-Anglican proportion of the country's population (Methodism itself having arisen from the Established Church). By 1851 they were the largest denomination among the Protestant Dissenters. Out of a total population of 16 million in England at that time, about $2\frac{1}{4}$ million attended Methodist services on Census Sunday 1851. The total attendance for all Protestant Dissenters was nearly $4\frac{1}{2}$ million. The number of Methodist has now declined, however, and in 1961 the total was some 600,000.

20. Western, p. 371f.

21. D. Bowen, *The Idea of the Victorian Church* (1968), p. 254.

22. Ibid., p. 251.

23. Winnington Ingram, *Work in Great Cities* (1896), p. 22.

24. Gay, p. 80.

25. Ibid., p. 98.

26. Ibid., p. 90.

27. London, Southwark, Manchester, Birmingham, Liverpool, Sheffield, Rochester, Wakefield, Durham, Chelmsford, Bristol and Portsmouth.

28. Leslie Paul, *The Development and Payment of the Clergy* (1964), p. 54.

29. Gay, p. 225, Table 6, based on the Newman Demographic Survey.

30. Roth, p. 261.

31. Paul, p. 26.

32. Paul, p. 11.

33. For this and the next suggested reason, together with supporting statistics and Note 34, as well as for other criticisms of this chapter, I am

indebted to Dr Robert Towler of the Sociology Department, University of Leeds.

34. Cf., for example, the case of the Dewsbury church which, even after consideration by the General Synod of the Church of England, was demolished rather than permit it to be sold to a non-Anglican immigrant congregation.

Part Two

Marx and Indian Religion

4. From Europe to India

IN Marx's view Christian theology was philosophically unsupportable, and Christian institutional religion, in its alliance with the Prussian state, was morally disreputable. This view of it rested upon the judgement that the state itself was disreputable, in that it was a bureaucratic organisation for promoting the interests of an élite and for safeguarding these interests against erosion by the interests of the majority of the people. To regard the state as disreputable for such a reason entails, obviously, a value judgement in favour of the interests of the majority of the people over against those of the élite minority.

Marx's own evaluation of the state had begun from his experience of its repressive nature, in the matter of the censorship of the press when the latter had ventured to criticise religion. His initial objection to the state was, therefore, that its position on this issue was based on two assumptions which nobody was allowed to challenge: first, that Christian doctrines about God, the world and man were true and beyond all criticism; second, that the state, in its own interests, had the right to uphold these doctrines with all the powers at its command. One could challenge neither the content of the doctrines nor the right of the state to uphold those doctrines by force if necessary.

Both these assumptions constituted a denial of the right of human beings to engage in free intellectual enquiry, and it was this which was the root of Marx's theoretical criticism of the state. The denial of free enquiry into the state's *right* to enforce acceptance of Christian ideas rendered all the more suspect the other area where free enquiry was forbidden, namely the credibility of Christian assertions. If these had to be defended by force, the conclusion was that they had no strength of their own by which to survive.

There was, however, a positive, alternative conclusion, namely that free enquiry into the nature of those religious ideas which were thus being defended by the state was regarded by the state as undesirable because it might reveal that coercive use was being made of religion by the state, and that this was not compatible with the fundamental and original character of the religion. If that were so, it would be a case of institutionalised forms of religion being defended by the state for the state's own purposes over against the judgement of those who were the genuine bearers and true representatives of the religious tradition itself. That is to say, religion would in such a case be receiving hypocritical, opportunist respect from the state for reasons best understood by state officials. The representatives and guardians of the religion would be, so to speak, the prisoners of the state, unable to prevent the prostitution of religion for political ends.

Now it is evident that such a situation would be likely to occur only when a state's power over religious leaders was entirely irresistible. In any other circumstances the religious leaders could dissent if they objected to what they regarded as the misuse of religion by the state. If they did not dissent when the state was thus making use of religion, it must be either because they concurred or because they did not recognise what was happening.

How often this may have happened in the history not only of Christianity but of other religions also, is an important question; for on the answers given will depend a deeper understanding of the political as well as 'spiritual' roles that various religions have played in world history. The question is one of assessing, for example, the extent to which the dominant forms of Christianity in the West have been conditioned by political 'protection'. The naïve assumption of believers is frequently that *their* religion is the true, politically unconditional form; rarely do adherents of the English Church acknowledge that the character of English Christianity is as much shaped by the interests of the English state as the historical continuation of an eastern-Mediterranean cult. What is demanded, and what is often given, is assent to the idea that the English form of Christianity is the same as the 'faith once delivered to the saints'. In hymnology this finds pious expression in such phrases as 'Thy hand, O God, has guided Thy Church from age to age'; it would be more appropriate to acknowledge that it more often has been someone else's hand which has guided the conditioning and shaping of the English Church. This is simply to draw attention to the gap which generally exists between professional historiography and popular piety.

In a similar way it becomes necessary to raise such questions with regard to other religions, and to try to assess the extent to which this has happened in the case of other 'great' religions which, although state-established and supported, are regarded by their adherents as faithfully preserving the original insight and attitudes of the founder. To attempt to answer such questions is one of the important tasks awaiting the comparative history and sociology of religion. It is a project not directly envisaged by Marx, but is nevertheless one which is in keeping with his analysis as the following words indicate:

> Technology discloses man's mode of dealing with nature, the process of production by which he sustains his life, and thereby also lays bare the mode of formation of his social relations and of the mental conceptions which flow from them. *Every history of religion even, that fails to take account of this material base, is uncritical.*[1]

It is this taking into account of the material and, one may add, social base which is most characteristic of Marx's method, and certainly it is this which distinguishes his approach from that of metaphysicians and speculative idealists who pay scant, if any, attention to the conditioning of social relations and ideas by material factors.

In the circumstances in which he lived, some of Marx's writing was inevitably polemical. Parts of his work, however, such as the *Economic and Philosophic Manuscripts of 1844*, are distinctly more penetrating and less polemical in mood and style than others such as *The Holy Family*. But even if some of his work was polemical, this does not detract from its value as a corrective to the unrealistic accounts of religion given by idealist philosophers and theologians, some of whom seem capable of becoming indefinitely lost in metaphysical space.

Certainly in the perspective of much of the writing on Indian religion by Western and westernised-Indian philosophers it is this kind of corrective that is needed. On the other hand, as the French anthropologist, Maurice Godelier, has recently put it, it is important not to be deceived by mere appearances, that is, 'the visible and spontaneous representation which members of a society derive from the nature of things, from their own activities or from the universe'. Instead, the more valuable method is initially to disregard the surface appearances of things and relationships 'not in order to leave them unexplained as if beyond any rational knowledge, but in order to come back to them later and, having discovered the inner relationships and sequences of things, explain them with this new knowledge'.[2] It is this penetration into the inner relationships between material, social and ideological factors which is most evidently lacking from conventional, 'traditional' accounts of religion, both Asian and Western, but especially Asian.

So far as Western religion is concerned there is now no lack of professional historians who have used this kind of perspective: Christopher

Hill, Eric Hobsbawm, V. G. Kiernan, E. P. Thompson, and many others. Among sociologists there is hardly one, as W. G. Runciman has commented, 'who is not a Marxist – who would not accept, that is, the propositions that men make their own history but not as they please, that ideology is conditioned by social structure, and that to understand the workings of any society it is necessary to understand how its form of social organisation relates to its stage of economic development'.[3]

Much less has been done in the sociological study of Asian religion to apply these propositions, either by Western or by Asian scholars, although some of the latter have now begun to examine their own traditions in this way. The rest of this chapter will be devoted to a brief exploration of the religious and non-religious factors which underlay the attitudes of the British to Indian religion in the nineteenth century, attitudes which have resulted in various and contradictory accounts of the nature of Indian religion which range from severe moral condemnation to idealistic rhapsodising.

(ii) *Citizens and Anglicans – in India*

In 1662, the same year that the Act of Parliament was passed which had the effect of declaring the entire English people to be one comprehensive religious-political system, namely the Church of England, the English fleet under the Earl of Marlborough arrived off Bombay and demanded the cession of the island from the Portuguese. Bombay had been secured in 1661 by Charles II as his possession through his marriage to Catherina of Braganza; this was the same year, incidentally, that he granted a new charter 'for ever' to the East India Company 'to make peace or war with any non-Christian prince or people' in India. Possession of Bombay would facilitate the business of the Company, which had by that time established factories at various places in India including Agra, and Ahmedabad, Balasor and Hooghly in Bengal, Madras, Patna, and the fabulously wealthy city of Surat. English Protestant clergymen had already been appointed as chaplains at these places. One such had been posted to Surat by the Directors of the East India Company as early as 1614. He had been commended to the Directors for his learning and gravity, and his ability to contest and hold arguments with the Jesuits who were already at that time well in evidence at Surat. However he was later relieved of his charge for unworthy conduct; as an Anglican bishop in India later observed, it was obvious that conditions at Surat, 'where everyone was absorbed in money-making can hardly have made the task of a Chaplain particularly easy'.[4]

English chaplains were going to India regularly by 1662, and a frequent injunction given them by the Directors of the Company was that they should not tolerate any interference with the Protestant religion. One of the chaplains appointed to Madras was a Mr Isaacson (son of a highly placed official in the City of London); in 1656 he received a despatch from the Court of Directors in England strictly requiring him not to 'permit or suffer the Catholic fathers to make processions or ceremonies or walking before any dead corpse with Bell, Book, Candle, Cross or any of them, or to baptise any English infants, or to visit any English that it shall please God to afflict with sickness, either in our Fort or within the town, thereby to confess or seduce them to their Popish vanities'.[5] Englishmen (and Englishwomen and English children) it was quite clear, could not in any circumstances, anywhere in the world be allowed to be religiously anything other than Church of England. The attempt was still being made to bring the entire population of England within one comprehensive religious-political institution, the Anglican Church.

Thus the nation which was engaged in the conquest of the land and people of India was officially and nominally not only 'Christian', but also Protestant and Anglican. What was entailed in Britain being a Christian country, in the latter part of the eighteenth century and the early part of the nineteenth, when the British occupation of India was carried out, was that the Church of England was the established church with the king as its Head, with bishops exercising their rights as Lords spiritual, and the Church of England incumbents taking their part in the work of regulating English society. Perhaps the most vigorous religious force in England at that time was the Clapham Sect, a group of Evangelicals who formed a very powerful pressure group both within Parliament and outside it. They were not strictly a 'sect' in the sociological sense, but a 'party' within the Church of England and with some sympathisers and supporters outside it.

Their ideological position was, briefly, as follows. They energetically supported British imperialism in India. They held that Christianity was the only true religion. The Church of England was the appropriate form of religious organisation for Englishmen, and was a bulwark against Roman Catholicism. It was mainly on these grounds that dissenting sects, who also held that Protestant Christianity was the one true religion over against all forms of heathen superstitition, were acceptable allies. The conversion of Hindus and other heathen people to Christianity would help to perpetuate British imperial rule in India. Moral reformation of a puritanical kind was urgently needed in India, as well as in Britain. It was needed in Britain, in the Evangelicals' view, as the answer to the continental Enlightenment, and to the French Revolution and similar kinds of atheistic ideology.[6] Britain was, therefore, in this view, a 'Christian' country (officially), and yet at the same time a country not worthy of the name Christian (actually). Their aim was to reduce the gap between the nominal and the actual condition of the English people.

Charles Grant, one of the leading members of the Evangelicals, expressed their point of view in a speech which he made in 1797, as a director of the East India Company.

> In considering the affairs of the world as under the control of the Supreme Disposer, and those distant territories . . . providentially put into our hands . . . is it not necessary to conclude that they were given to us, not merely that we might draw an annual profit from them, but that we might diffuse among their inhabitants, long sunk in darkness, vice and misery, the light and benign influence of the truth, the blessings of a well-regulated society. . . .[7]

Evidently Grant considered that Britain *was* Christian in the sense that the nation's imperialistic commercial enterprises met with the approval of the Christian God. 'The blessings of a well-regulated society' could hardly, however, be a reference to eighteenth-century 'Christian' England, but rather to some Evangelical ideal which Grant and his fellow Claphamites cherished personally. For many of the working people of England at that time were themselves, as Grant, Wilberforce and the other Evangelicals knew well, 'sunk in darkness, vice and misery' (in Claphamite terms), and were, before the end of the nineteenth century, going to sink even deeper. London, a mere fraction then of its present size (Clapham was then a quiet stockbroker-belt suburb), swarmed, we are told, with 50,000 prostitutes and hundreds of pimps, who 'made their living by getting females from eleven to fourteen years old for prostitution'.[8]

Nevertheless England was at that time a 'Christian' country, according to the religious partisan propagandists of today. Whatever else such a statement may mean, it has to be accepted that in nineteenth-century England's case it meant to have developed a form of society in which military aggression, commercial imperialism, the uncontrolled appetite for the accumulation of private wealth, and the prostitution of women appear to have been closely associated.

The erosion of Anglicanism in the nineteenth century was accomplished by increasing efforts to convert to Christianity the people of Britain's conquered territories overseas. This was closely related to a movement of evangelical revivalism which coincided approximately with Anglican decline. The rapid growth in the number of adherents to Methodism in the first hundred years of that movement's history added considerably to the non-Anglican proportion of the country's population. By 1851 they were the largest religious denomination of non-Anglicans in England. Out of a total population of 16 million about $2\frac{1}{4}$ million attended Methodist services on Census Sunday 1851. The total attendance for all Protestant Dissenters was nearly $4\frac{1}{2}$ million. E. J. Hobsbawm describes the situation in predominantly Protestant countries, especially in the United States and Britain in the late eighteenth century, in terms of 'mass religious revivalism of hysterical intensity, in which men and women could find a welcome release from the stresses of a society which provided no equivalent outlets for mass emotion, and destroyed those which had existed in the past'.[9] In a society which is being industrialised, sects spring up from at least two major causes present in such a situation. One is the personal emotional disturbance, individually deep and socially wide-spread, which industrialisation produces; the other is the facility for forming sects which a congested urban area presents as compared with rural life; in the former people have a greater chance of being able to form *ad hoc* social groups with others having the same problems and attitudes.

In England, where Anglicans had lost some of their *direct* religious monopoly, it was possible from the middle of the eighteenth century onwards for sectarian religion, of the kind which the Wesleyan revival produced, to find open expression. In some European continental countries where there was no scope for openly acknowledged sectarian movements, protest against the monopoly religion of the established Church took the form of a mass withdrawal from any form of religion in the direction of positive secularism.[10]

A counter-culture is, in principle, a criticism of the culture out of which it arises and a protest against it. It is therefore, inevitably, in some sense and to some extent a threat to the major culture. In the case of Methodist revivalism, and the associated Evangelicalism which extended beyond Methodism proper, the force of the protest was partly blunted and partly deflected. It was blunted by what Kiernan has shown to have been the success of the developing sections of the middle classes in capturing religious enthusiasm and making it a support of civil order and stability.[11] After the end of the eighteenth century, two types of religion existed in uneasy coexistence in England; one was *nominal* or formal religion, that of the established Church; the other was called by its adherents, *vital* religion. Between these two conceptions of religion the French Revolution, just across the Channel, made it imperative for those with a conservative interest in English society to choose. 'One (conception) was of religion as the formulary of an established society, its statement of faith in itself; the other as a catastrophic conversion of the individual, a miraculous shaking off of secret burdens. One was fixed on this world, the other on the next.'[12] One was the conception of religion largely held until then by the upper classes, and given elegant expression by Burke; the other was the religion (in so far as they had any) of the depressed working classes of the new industrial slums. It was necessary, therefore, in order to promote social stability, to head off the potential threat of revolution by preventing this religious expression of distress from developing into a political critique. It became necessary 'that upper and lower classes should find common ground, that they should believe the same things. At any rate a proportion of the upper classes should join heartily in belief, and the rest should make a better pretence of doing so.'[13] It was this that William Wilberforce and others like him achieved. Although Wilberforce had undergone religious conversion before 1789, 'it required the Revolution to make a religious propagandist of him . . . . What was emotionally necessary to him, he could recommend to others as politically necessary.' He was quite prepared to state the political arguments for the upper classes becoming involved in Evangelical religion, and to do so openly, as he himself said in a book published in the closing years of the eighteenth century, entitled *A Practical View of the Prevailing Religious System of Professed Christians in the Higher and Middle Classes in this Country, Contrasted with Real Christianity*; his intention was 'to suggest inferior motives to readers, who might be less disposed to listen to considerations of a higher order'.[14]

(iii) *Revivalism and foreign missions*

So it was that Wilberforce and his associates in the Clapham Sect succeeded in capturing the revivalist, religious counter-culture and rendering it politically innocuous. At the same time that lower-class protest was thus blunted, it was also deflected; before it could direct any of its force against the religious and social establishment of England it was canalised in another direction, namely against the heathen in far-off foreign lands. Perhaps it was sheer coincidence that Christian missionaries from Britain began their efforts in real earnest just at the time when they could only appear to many Asians as, in R. C. Zaehner's words, 'the spiritual representatives of the imperialists'.[15] Zaehner points out the further coincidence that English Protestant missions were launched at a time when European rationalists were beginning their intellectual assault on all religious belief. It was a time when orthodox Christian belief in an almighty God was being severely shaken by the confident advance of scientific knowledge; the faith of those of the eduated middle classes, who were of more reasonable disposition and therefore more susceptible to the virus of doubt, was becoming depressed and needed reviving. Evangelical missions to the heathen of distant Africa and Asia provided the occasion for much virtuous activity, in the pursuit of which selfish doubts and fears could be forgotten. 'Those activities, thousands of miles away from home, recaptured for the body politic its good conscience, its moral faith in itself in spite of sedition trials, famine wages, and French victories.'[16] It has to be noted that this concern for missions to the heathen was in spite of the fact that the mass of people of England (the vast majority of whom were untouched even by the Methodist revival) were, by the beginning of the nineteenth century, outside the pale of organised Christianity.

Four new missionary societies were founded in Britain between 1792 and 1804: the Baptist Missionary Society (1792), the interdenominational London Missionary Society (1795), the evangelical Church Missionary Society (1799) and the British and Foreign Bible Society (1804). As the industrialisation of England was intensified and foreign wars of colonial conquest extended the British army to the point of embarrassment with so many commitments, so the tempo of converting the heathen was stepped up, or more accurately, of *attempting* to convert the heathen, for even as late as 1931, after more than a century of missionary activity, only 1.5 per cent of the population of British India, including Burma, were Christians.[17] Nevertheless, missionary activity had a great effect on the senders, however little it had on the recipients. Confronted with militarily defeated, materially dispossessed non-Christian populations, they were able to feel great confidence, as K. M. de Silva has put it, 'that theirs was a creed which surpassed all others'; they were enabled to believe that theirs was a winning cause, 'that their efforts at proselytism must certainly culminate in the triumph of Christianity at the expense of all other religions'.[18] They were greatly encouraged in their efforts by Evangelicals in government posts in England, such as Lord Glenelg, the Secretary of State for the Colonies, who was 'greatly interested in the conversion of the heathen', and James Stephen, the Permanent Under Secretary at the Colonial Office, a distinguished member of the Clapham Sect whose personal influence in that office was continually being exerted in the cause of converting the inhabitants of Britain's colonies to evangelical Christianity.[19]

In the course of promoting and conducting foreign missions decade after decade through the nineteenth century, the evangelicals responsible for such activity (and the base in the home churches was constantly being expanded whenever possible) naturally grew accustomed to the view that Christianity was the *supreme* truth among other lesser versions (to put it modestly) or, less modestly, the *only* truth, all other faiths being but 'darkness' and 'the power of Satan', as the Yorkshireman, R. Spence Hardy, described Buddhist life in a book entitled *The British Government and the Idolatry of Ceylon*.[20] Evangelical Christianity thus moved easily into the position of a monopoly ideology. Nor was such confidence in Christianity as the sole truth for all men shown only abroad: in England there was founded in 1813 the 'London Society for Promoting Christianity among the Jews' of which no less a person than the Duke of Kent became Chairman.

Nevertheless, in the actual encounter with the 'heathen' the experience of the Westerner was not always one of confident superiority to illiterate, superstitious and benighted savages. Some missionaries acknowledged the high quality of the belief systems of Asian peoples and of the lives of those who adhered to them. Others recognised that these systems possessed admirable qualities in *theory*, but emphasised that the *practice* of the heathen was vicious and terrible. The ferocity with which they affirmed the latter made up for any concessions they may have made when regarding the former.[21]

Thus the counter-culture of early nineteenth-century salvation religion was successfully harnessed and brought into the service of the expanding, industrial, colonial British state. The legacy of this control and redirection of the counter-culture by those with an interest in conserving the existing political and cultural structure was the growth of a permanent attitude of absolute superiority, on the part of the majority of Protestant Christians, towards any Asian belief system. The principle of ideological monopoly had in the end been stengthened.

Christian missionary activity in India in the first half of the nineteenth century had thus served two major political purposes for the British. First it had prevented lower-class religious expressions of distress from finding political expression by diverting them into what became a steadily growing evangelical concern for the supposedly *spiritually* impoverished peoples of India. Second it had, by the middle of the century, provided the

Englishmen who were being recruited into the East India Company's service with a well-developed view of their own undoubted cultural superiority to the benighted Indians, whose land and wealth they were to administer in the interest of the British commercial classes. It was the prospect of material gain which attracted the British to India in the seventeenth century; it was territorial conquest in the eighteenth and early nineteenth centuries which greatly enlarged the possibilities of such material gain; and it was, finally, by a conviction of their cultural mission to the people of India that they justified the enterprise by the middle decades of the nineteenth century.

This sense of cultural superiority felt by the British produced a reaction, however, among Indians, and especially among the higher castes. These had also, by the middle of the nineteenth century, learnt to take a new pride in their own religious and cultural tradition. This new pride, as it happened, was stimulated by the British presence in India, for at the end of the eighteenth century the policy of the East India Company had not been favourable to missionary activity in its territories. The conception of religion held by the upper classes in England, mentioned earlier and typified in the writings and speeches of Burke, found full expression in the person of Lord Wellesley, who was appointed to take charge of British interests in India in 1798. The idea that each country had its dominant religion, adhered to by all its people, and that in Britain this was Protestantism, had as its corollary that in India the dominant religion happened to be, so far as could be seen, the religion of the Hindus, or as Westerners began to call it (by analogy with Protestantism, Catholicism etc.), 'Hinduism'. This being so, it was argued by the aristocratic administrator, if there should arise a need to strengthen religious forces in India it would be to 'Hinduism' that attention would appropriately be directed.

(iv) *Countering insurrection: the Vedantic revival*

This, then, was the policy followed by Lord Wellesley almost from the moment of his arrival in Calcutta in 1798. From his point of view there were, at that time, cogent reasons for the British to encourage and strengthen every possible agency of stability and conservation in Indian life. For the Mughal empire had been in decline since the death of Aurangzeb in 1707 and was now in ruins, having lost whatever capacity it might once have had for preserving law and order and providing cultural cohesion even in northern India. The French Revolution had provided a recent ugly example of the form which anti-conservative forces could take, and in the East generally the French were England's most dangerous rivals. And whereas the evangelical movement in England and its foreign missionary outreach may have effected a diversion of dangerous popular expression of material distress, in India its effects might seriously jeopardise the situation. For in India, too, there were popular movements, often associated with religious elements, which threatened to disrupt law and order. There had, for example, been a number of revolts and insurrections in various parts of Bengal in the years immediately preceding Wellesley's arrival: in Rangpur in 1783, in Bankura in 1789, in Midnapur in 1795. Against these and other similar movements of popular unrest, effective counter-measures would have to be taken quickly. Not for nothing had Wellesley, a year or so earlier, made a brilliant speech in the House of Commons against the dangers threatened by the revolution in France; the brother of the Duke of Wellington, Wellesley was a man not only of words but of action. In Calcutta, however, he quickly came to appreciate that the campaign in which he was engaged was partly administrative and partly ideological.

Popular religion in Bengal at the end of the eighteenth century could not be relied upon as an ally of conservatism and stability. It was necessary to look elsewhere, to something more politically reliable than the *vital* religion of the lower classes. He was not long in finding the answer. It lay in the scholarly and philosophical traditions of Brāhmanism, enshrined in the ancient Sanskritic texts which were still preserved and studied by the pundits of Benares and Nabadwip. Wellesley decided that in future such learning should be promoted more energetically in Calcutta, and conceived the brilliant plan of combining this with the need to have a centre where the East India Company's young officers, as they arrived in Bengal, might acquire the kind of familiarity with Indian language and culture which would enable them to become efficient administrators.

Thus, in 1800, he founded the College of Fort William in Calcutta which was, according to his Minute dated 10 July of that year, 'to fix sound and correct principles of religion and government' as 'the best security which could be provided for the stability of British power in India'. It would thus provide the necessary antidote to revolutionary ideas and activities. One of the important steps in the carrying out of this policy was to gather Sanskrit pundits to Calcutta, and to enlist the support of influential members of the Brāhman caste. This latter objective would certainly not be achieved if they were alienated from British rule by the crude attacks on Hindu religion made by Christian missionaries. Hence, the attitude of those British officials who were responsible for *administering* Indian territory differed from that of the missionaries whose concern was to propagate Christianity. Many of the officials, as E. D. Potts has written, 'were rightly convinced that an insurrection would result if missionaries were allowed to promote their ends willy-nilly' and that 'widespread unrest, terminating British rule, would certainly follow in the wake of the ideas the missionaries were to spread'.[22]

The official policy was, therefore, to encourage as far as possible the reform of Hindu religion from within, and to stimulate its milder and more 'spiritual' elements so as to mitigate the cruder and more brutal aspects which were perennially the targets of missionary scorn. In a sense this policy succeeded very well; even, in a sense, too well in the long run, for the reinstatement of Sanskritic culture and the modernised veneer which Hindu religion received in the nineteenth century became for caste Hindus not only the source of new pride in their native culture but also, by the closing decades of the century, the basis of a growing Hindu nationalism. But of this there was little sign throughout the first half of the century.

The Hindu reformers, the revivers of what they held to be the 'pure' Vedic culture of the Sanskritic holy books, had to contend with opposition from their own more conservative fellow-Hindus. One of the most outstanding of the reformers and revitalisers was Ram Mohun Roy, who is generally regarded now as the father of the modern Vedantic form of caste Hindu religion. Ram Mohun Roy was a Brāhman landowner who had grown rich in the conditions created by British rule, notably by the Permanent Settlement of 1793 which resulted in a considerable redistribution of the ownership of land in Bengal. Of his many activities there is no need to write here as the literature on Ram Mohun is very extensive;[23] more has been written about him than possibly any other single figure in the nineteenth-century history of India. He was a rich man, a man who by the time he was forty could afford to be a man of leisure and scholarship. He entered the service of the East India Company not for the salary he would receive but rather for the opportunity it would afford him of 'learning the English language and studying the English character'.[24] One important lesson he learnt from Digby, the District Magistrate of Rangpur with whom he worked, was a new evaluation of the French Revolution. Digby found that Ram Mohun had a great admiration for the revolutionaries; it was not too difficult, however, to persuade him of the dangers of this attitude when it was pointed out to him what the possible consequences of such ideas might be if they were allowed to spread among the people of India. His admiration then turned to detestation.[25]

Ram Mohun became the founder and leader of a movement of Hindu reform, known eventually as the Brahmo Samaj (the Spiritual, or Godly, Society), most of whose members were, like himself, from the upper castes, and many of whom were wealthy landowners and entrepreneurs. One who was closely associated with Ram Mohun was Dwarkanath Tagore (grandfather of Rabindranath) whose wealth gained him the honorary title of 'Prince' and who, when he visited England, was received by Queen Victoria. The Brahmo movement had as one of its major purposes the eradication of what were regarded by its members as the idolatrous practices of the mass of the Hindus, and the replacement of crude materialistic ideas and attitudes – which owed not a little, in late eighteenth – and early nineteenth-century Bengal, to vulgarised forms of Tantra – by the refined and spiritual truths of Vedantic philosophy. One of the objections to popular Hindu religious practice voiced by Ram Mohun was that it entailed the diversion of wealth from already hard-pressed, Government-taxed peasantry into the hands of village priests. Ram Mohun was also concerned about the fact that landholders (such as himself) were not receiving a fair share of the amount collected in land tax from the peasants.[26]

Ram Mohun co-operated with the imperial rulers in many ways, advising them on proposals for reform of the law touching Hindu traditional practices such as *satī*.[27] He also visited England on behalf of the Mughal Emperor, in order to make representations before the British Government for an increased allowance for this old pensioner of the British. It was for this service that he received the honorary feudal title of *Raja* in August 1829.

The Vedantic philosophy which, in Fort William College and by the Brahmo Samaj, was now being revived and given a prominence it had not had for centuries, was one of the six ancient schools of Brāhmanical thought. Some of these classical systems were of a materialist kind, as Debiprasad Chattopadhyaya has shown, and there are, in addition, other avowedly materialistic philosophies which are undeniably as much a part of the Indian heritage as the anti-materialism of the Vedanta.[28] But if a view of the world was required which would divert men's attention from material concerns and direct it instead to the pure eternal world of the spirit, or *brāhman*, to a realm of being where material things fade into insignificance and are seen as merely *maya*, illusion, then no better choice could possibly be made than the philosophy of Vedanta. For Vedantic sophistry has an unbounded capacity for endowing with a halo of sanctity that which in other systems of thought and by other standards of logic and reason would be regarded as meaningless assertions.

The success achieved by the British aristocratic rulers of Bengal and their aristocratic Indian collaborators in promoting widespread acceptance of Vedanta was not immediate. The Brahmo Samaj remained for long a movement having a limited, sophisticated, upper-class appeal. Nevertheless its influence spread more widely as the years went by; by the end of the nineteenth century it had certainly helped very substantially to secure a new status for its purified Vedantic Hinduism, and also for the idea that Indian culture was at heart deeply spiritual while that of the West was grossly materialistic.

By the middle of the century, however, when Marx turned his attention for a while to the Indian scene, it had not become a sufficiently prominent feature for him to be aware of it. The more characteristic view of Hindu culture among Europeans was of a kind which the following passages from a missionary writer, quoted by M. Wylie, a Calcutta judge, in 1854, well exemplify:

'Hinduism, as is well known, is not only a system of false religion, but a system of false science . . . .'. Nevertheless, the writer continued, the young Bengali was often remarkably intelligent. At his first glimpse of the science and knowledge, 'scales seemed to have fallen from his eyes; he felt giddy and intoxicated with the changed appearance of all things. But if there was one feeling stronger than all others, and which for a time reigned predominant, it was a passionate loathing, a mixture of hatred and contempt and indignation, against the superstition in which he had been brought up. When he thought of the absurdities he had been led to believe, of the pain and misery he had been compelled to bear and to inflict, of the clay and wooden images and rabble of so-called deities whom he had worshipped; of the ignorance in which he had been kept; and its results in making every other Hindu a mere beast of burden for the Brahman; and when he looked at all in the light of his new-found knowldge, he blushed with shame and indignation, and felt that he had been injured and humiliated and degraded.'[29]

This was the kind of assessment of Hindu religion's tenuous hold on the minds of young, Western-educated Bengalis which accorded well with Marx's confidence concerning the inevitable collapse of religious attitudes once they were exposed to Western scientific learning, and provided they were not given artifical respiration by the state for its own purposes. It was a view of religion common in the middle and latter decades of the nineteenth century. But it was not supported, as we shall see, in the case of Aurobindo Ghose in the first decade of the twentieth century.

NOTES

1. Marx and Engels, *On Religion*, p. 122 (emphasis added).
2. Maurice Godelier, *Perspectives in Marxist Anthropology,* trans. by Robert Brain (1977), p. 3.
3. *Times Literary Supplement* (16 January 1976), p. 46.
4. Eyre Chatterton, *A History of the Church of England in India Since the Early Days of the East India Company* (1924), p. 13.
5. Ibid., p. 22.
6. F. K. Brown, *Father of the Victorians: the Age of Wilberforce* (1961).
7. M. Edwards, *Asia in the European Age* (1961), p. 109.
8. Brown, p. 25.
9. E. J. Hobsbawm, *The Age of Revolution* (1962).
10. Ibid., p. 268.
11. V. G. Kiernan, 'Evangelicalism and the French Revolution', in *Past and Present*, vol. I (1952).
12. Ibid., p. 46.
13. Ibid.
14. Ibid., p. 48.
15. R. C. Zaehner, *The Catholic Church and World Religions* (1964), p. 11.
16. Kiernan, p. 52.
17. *Census of India, 1931.*
18. K. M. De Silva, *Social Policy and Missionary Organisations in Ceylon, 1840–1855* (1956), p. 282.
19. Ibid., pp. 24–26.
20. R. Spence Hardy, *The British Government and the Idolatry of Ceylon* (1841), p. 6.
21. Helen G. Trager, *Burma Through Alien Eyes* (1966), chap. VII.
22. E. Daniel Potts, *British Baptist Missionaries in India, 1793–1837* (1967), p. 170.
23. The standard biography is by Sophie Collet, *The Life and Letters of Raja Rammohun Roy* (1900; repub. 1961).
24. Nivanjan Dhar. *Vedanta and Bengal Renaissance* (1977), p. 41.
25. Ibid. p. 47.

26. *Exposition on Judicial and Revenue Systems of India* (1833), no. IV, quoted by Dhar, p. 50. See also *Ram Mohun Roy on Indian Economy*, edited by Susobhan Chandra Sarkar (1965), p. 25, para 18.

27. The self-immolation of a Hindu widow on her husband's funeral pyre.

28. See D. Chattopadhyaya, *Indian Atheism* and *Lokayata: A Study in Ancient Indian Materialism* (1959).

29. M. Wylie, *Bengal as a Field of Mission* (1854), p. 148.

5 Marx and Indian Religion

(i) *Marx's studies of India*

IN so far as Marx extended his researches in history and society beyond Europe, it was to India, if anywhere, that he devoted a certain amount of special attention. It has to be remembered that at that time 'India' covered what today is Pakistan and Bangladesh as well as the modern republic of India; parts of Burma also had already become a province of British India when Marx was writing.

His interest in India arose from his work as the London correspondent of the *New York Daily Tribune*. He undertook this work at a time when he and his family were living in London in conditions of extreme poverty. They had arrived in London in August 1849; in the course of the events in Paris following the 1848 revolution and its collapse, Marx had been given twenty hours' notice by the police to leave Paris. In the hope that the increasingly reactionary nature of the French Government meant another revolutionary uprising in France before long, he had consulted Engels on his plans for the immediate future and decided to go to London. His wife Jenny and their three small children were to follow as soon as it could be arranged. This was not easy for they had practically no funds. But with the help of Jenny's mother they were able, eventually, to rent a two-roomed flat in Chelsea where the family installed themselves just three weeks before the birth of Jenny's fourth child, Heinrich, on 5 November. 'While the people outside were shouting "Guy Fawkes for ever!". . . and all was in an uproar, my poor little Heinrich was born. We call him Little Fawkes in honour of the great conspirator', Jenny wrote in her memoirs.[1]

After about six months the family had to leave this flat as they were again without money. The bailiffs sequestered their few possessions, 'everything, even my poor child's cradle and the best toys of my daughters who stood there weeping bitterly', wrote Jenny. She and her children were left to lie on the bare floor and the next morning they left; eventually, with the help of a German refugee friend, they found a room elsewhere.

The story of the Marx family in London continues in the same strain. The Marx family saw Victorian, imperial Britain from the underside. The child, Heinrich, died when he was a year old. Another child, a daughter born soon after, died three weeks later. What saved the family from total disaster was the constant help they received from Friedrich Engels, Marx's life-long friend. In 1852, however, at the invitation of the editor of the *New York Daily Tribune*, Charles Dana, Marx became one of the paper's foreign correspondents and from then onwards for about ten years he contributed a series of regular weekly articles. In this respect also Engels used to help him out whenever he found it impossible to complete his piece in time for it to catch the mail-steamer from Liverpool.

As London correspondent his concern was with the whole range of British affairs, and particularly with matters which would specially interest readers of the *Tribune*. The paper had a reputation for progressive, even radical policies: anti-slavery, anti-colonialism, and what Marx described as 'philanthropic socialistic anti-industrialism' were some of its major characteristic concerns. So India and the activities of the British in that great land were naturally the kind of topics that would interest its readers, especially since the American States themselves had, eighty years or so earlier, succeeded in throwing off British colonial rule.

It happened, moreover, that in 1853 the Charter of the East India Company was about to become due for renewal for a further twenty years. Originally the Charter granted by the British Government had given the Company the right to the monopoly of trade with India and China, to govern India and to levy taxes. In 1813 the Company's monopoly of trade in India had been ended, but the right to govern its territories in India was retained. The Company operated through a Board of Directors, and there were in 1853 proposals for changing the Board's constitution. This reform as it was intended to be, did not, however, in Marx's view, amount to very much compared with the major issue. For again and again in his articles on India Marx emphasises that it is the *people* of England who bore the burden of taxes to meet the cost of the administration of Britain's Indian empire, while it was the merchant class who made themselves rich on the goods they transferred from India to Britain. But revolution was in the air in Europe in the 1840s and 1850s, and might even break out in England. 'The English obligarchy have a presentiment of the approaching end of their days', wrote Marx in the first of his articles dealing with India, 'and they have a very justifiable desire to conclude such a treaty with English legislation, that even in the case of England's escaping from their weak and rapacious bands, they shall retain for themselves and their associates the privilege of plundering India for the space of 20 years.'[2]

Some of his material Marx found in the reports of current parliamentary proceedings. Other material, and by far the greater amount, he obtained from the long hours of library research he spent in the reading room of the

British Museum. During this period he was living near the Museum, in Dean Street, Soho, an area which attracted many continental refugees. For a time he and Engels became engrossed in the study of Asian society and history, and Engels even began to learn Persian,[3] a language which, until the beginning of the nineteenth century, had been used extensively in official circles in India.

Marx's historical knowledge of the non-European world was, according to Hobsbawm, 'not impressive on the ancient or medieval Middle East, but markedly better on certain parts of Asia, notably India'.[4] S. Avineri remarks that 'his understanding of Chinese society seems less profound than his grasp of Indian affairs'.[5] Similarly V. G. Kiernan comments that Marx 'offers generalizations about Asia that would be more convincing if restricted to India'.[6] If, then, India (that is to say, British India of the mid-nineteenth century) was the area of Asia which Marx had studied more thoroughly than other parts, it is important for our purpose to know how far his studies took him into the realm of religion and whether here, too, the criticism of religion was 'the premise of all criticism'; more generally, what potential for radical change he saw in the Indian subcontinent at that time.

(ii) *Marx on Indian religion*

In one of his earliest articles for the *New York Daily Tribune* he draws attention to the striking contrasts found in the religion of what he correctly refers to as 'Hindustan', a term which in itself is evidence of the subcontinent's two major cultural traditions, Hindu and Muslim:

> Hindustan is an Italy of Asiatic dimensions, the Himalayas for the Alps, the Plains of Bengal for the Plains of Lombardy, the Deccan for the Apennines, and the Isle of Ceylon for the Island of Sicily. The same rich variety in the products of the soil, and the same dismemberment in the political configuration. Just as Italy has, from time to time, been compressed by the conqueror's sword into different national masses, so do we find Hindustan, when not under the pressure of the Mohammedan, or the Mogul, or the Briton, dissolved into as many independent and conflicting States as it numbered towns, or even villages. Yet, in a social point of view, Hindustan is not the Italy, but the Ireland of the East. And this strange combination of Italy and of Ireland, of a world of voluptuousness and of a world of woes, is anticipated in the ancient traditions of the religion of Hindustan. That religion is at '

once a religion of sensualist exuberance, and a religion of self-torturing
asceticism; a religion of the Lingam and the Juggernaut; the religion of
the Monk, and of the Bayadere.[7]

The items which he selects for mention here are in fact all Hindu; it is the
contrast *within* Hindu religion which impresses him; not the contrast
between Hindu and Muslim religion, even though he refers to 'the
Mohammedan invasion' in the next paragraph. But he appears to have
regarded Hindu culture as the one continuing and abiding element. *All*
these invasions and conquests, he declares, did not penetrate below the
surface of Indian society: 'The loss of his old world, with no gain of a new
one, imparts a particular kind of melancholy to the present misery of the
Hindu, and separates Hindustan, ruled by Britain, from all its ancient
traditions, and from the whole of its past history.'[8]

The 'old world' to which he here refers is that of the entirely self-
contained village community, an idea which he accepted from his
European sources as having been the prevailing type of social formation in
pre-British India. We shall return to this later; meanwhile we note a further
characteristic of the religion of India which Marx mentions in this
connection: 'We must not forget that these little communities', he wrote,
'. . . subjugated man to external circumstances instead of elevating man
to be the sovereign of circumstances, that they transformed a self-
developing social state into never-changing natural destiny, and thus
brought about a brutalising worship of nature, exhibiting its degradation
in the fact that man, the sovereign of nature, fell down on his knees in
adoration of Hanuman, the monkey, and Sabbala, the cow.'[9]

Hindu religion is mentioned again in passing, in a polemical reference to
English religious hypocrisy: '. . . while they [the English] combated the
French revolution under the pretext of defending "our holy religion", did
they not forbid, at the same time, Christianity to be propagated in India,
and did they not, in order to make money out of the pilgrims streaming to
the temples of Orissa and Bengal, take up the trade in the murder and
prostitution perpetrated in the temple of Juggernaut'? Marx is here
referring to the famous temple near Puri, in Orissa, dedicated to the
worship of one of the Hindu deities, a form of the god Vishnu. The
reference is to the fact that 'the priests of the temple who were under the
protection of the East India Company, reaped immense profits from mass
pilgrimage while at the same time encouraging temple prostitution, and
from pompous festivities which were accompanied by the suicide and self-
torture of fanatical believers.'[10]

The Hindus have by their religion, Marx notes in another article, been made 'virtuosi in the art of self-torturing'. He refers to the Juggernaut festivals as 'the bloody rites of a religion of cruelty'.[11] This is in connection with the atrocities of the Mutiny of 1857, but Marx notes also that the British, by the methods of torture which they had used in the course of their administration of India, also bore a large responsibility: 'If the English could do these things in cold blood, is it surprising that the insurgent Hindus should be guilty, in the fury of revolt and conflict, of the crimes and cruelties alleged against them?'[12] It seems that Marx generally used the term Hindu in a precise sense; he does not use it simply to mean any native inhabitant of Hindustan of whatever religion, for in passages other than those which have been quoted he distinguishes between Hindus and 'Mohammedans'[13] (that is, Muslims). Similarly Engels distinguished between Hindus and Sikhs.[14] It appears, therefore, that in his references to religion in India, Marx dealt only with *Hindu* religion in the normally accepted special sense of the term. One positive explanation of his silence concerning the other religious communities, especially the Muslims, might be his reference to all previous invaders of India before the British having been 'Hinduised: Arabs, Turks, Tartars, Moguls, who had successively overrun India, soon became *Hinduised*, the barbarian conquerors being, by an eternal law of history, conquered themselves by the superior civilisation of their subjects'.[15] When, therefore, he makes a criticism of the religion of *Hindustan* (that is, India) it is the religion of the Hindu community specifically that he describes, but since, in his view, this type of religion had communicated its essential features to Muslim life in India also, there is no necessity to provide any separate account of the religion of India's Muslims. This is the conclusion which one is forced to draw from the evidence of Marx's writings on the subject; whether such a view is defensible is altogether another matter.

In essence, in Marx's view, the religion of Hindustan was a religion natural and appropriate to primitive village communities. A large question therefore arises at this point, namely how far was Marx's view of the religion of India empirically based, and how far was it the product of Marx's own theory or even supposition? In those matters where he is most specific he appears to be relying on the kind of account of Hindu religion given by most of the Western writers on India in the early nineteenth century, especially in the matter of the contrasting features: sensuality and cruelty; temple prostitution and ascetic self-torture. Reference to what are known to have been some of Marx's sources confirm this.[16]

However Marx did not confine himself entirely to the construction of an account of Indian religion based on information from contemporary writers. He ventured into theoretical explanation of some of its features. He explained Hindu sensuality and cruelty as the natural consequence of a stagnant type of social organisation, namely the primitive village republics which he believed to be the basis of the Asiatic mode of production.

The concept of an 'Asiatic mode of production' was one which Marx arrived at on the basis of his researches in Indian history and society, in the light of the earlier use of the same idea by Richard Jones, John Stuart Mill and others.[17] Our concern here is with the type of religion which, according to Marx, was associated with the Asiatic mode of production and its village communities, communities which were now, he observed, approaching their dissolution.

> These small stereotype forms of social organism have been to the greater part dissolved, and are disappearing, not so much through the brutal interference of the British tax-gatherer and the British soldier, as to the working of English steam and English free trade. Those family communities were based on domestic industry, in that peculiar combination of hand-weaving, hand-spinning and hand-tilling agriculture which gave them self-supporting power. English interference having placed the spinner in Lancashire and the weaver in Bengal, or sweeping away both Hindu spinner and weaver, dissolved these small semi-barbarian, semi-civilised communities, by blowing up their economical basis, and thus produced the greatest, and, to speak the truth, the only *social* revolution ever heard of in Asia.[18]

In their classical form these primitive communities had provided the perfect foundation for Oriental despotism, for 'they restrained the human mind within the smallest possible compass, making it the unresisting tool of superstition, enslaving it beneath traditional rules, depriving it of all grandeur and historical energies'. In its classical form it was in fact a 'barbarian egotism which, concentrating on some miserable patch of land had quietly witnessed the ruin of empires, the perpetration of unspeakable cruelties, the massacre of the population of large towns, with no other consideration bestowed on them than on natural events, itself the helpless prey of any aggressor who deigned to notice it at all'.[19] His account of the religious characteristics of the primitive communities is as follows:

> Those ancient social organisms of production are, as compared with bourgeois society, extremely simple and transparent. But they are

founded either on the immature development of man individually, who has not yet severed the umbilical cord that unites him with his fellow men in a primitive tribal community, or upon direct relations of subjection. They can arise and exist only when the development of the productive power of labour has not risen beyond a low stage, and when, therefore, the social relations within the sphere of material life, between man and man, and between man and nature, are correspondingly narrow. This narrowness is reflected in the ancient worship of nature, and in the other elements of the popular religions. The religious reflex of the real world can, in any case, only then finally vanish, when the practical relations of every-day life offer to man none but perfectly intelligible and reasonable relations with regard to his fellowmen and to nature.

The life-process of society, which is based on the process of material production, does not strip off its mystical veil until it is treated as production by freely associated men, and is consciously regulated by them in accordance with a settled plan. This, however, demands for society a certain material groundwork or set of conditions of existence which in their turn are the spontaneous product of a long and painful process of development.[20]

The significant features of the situation, as Marx sees them, are that men are still united with one another in social organisms of production which politically have the form either of primitive tribal communities, or of subjection to a despotic ruler. They are characterised not only by 'a low level of development of the productive power of labour' but also by limited relations within the sphere of material life, both 'between man and man and between man and Nature'. Not until the life process of society becomes that of 'freely associated men' will the 'mystical veil' hanging over it, which is religion, be stripped off. Only when the practical relations of everyday life consist of intelligible and reasonable relations between men, and between men and Nature, will the religious halo, the religious reflection of the improperly understood world, the mystical veil which otherwise hangs over life, disappear. But this will happen only after 'a long and painful process of development'.

It seems that in this passage Marx envisages the process of development towards a rational, religion-free social formation as one which is everywhere unilinear. But through what stages? This is a difficult question which the alleged existence of an Asiatic mode of production has raised for Marxist theory. The main stages of development towards a socialist society according to Marx are well known: from the ancient mode through the fuedal to the bourgeois–capitalist, and thus eventually to socialism. Where among these stages of development the Asiatic mode of production fits in is not clear. Does the Indian example suggest that it is possible to progress from the Asiatic mode directly to bourgeois-capitalist society?

(iii) *The fallacy of the unchanging, self-contained village republics*

It is unnecessary to pursue this question, since the idea of the Asiatic mode of production as a distinct type of economic formation appears to have been a misconception. Marx's account of it in Indian terms was derived largely from the report by Sir Charles Metcalfe, a British administrator in India, to a Select Committee of the House of Commons in 1832. Marx's sources of information about Indian society were not confined to Metcalfe's report,[21] but it was the 'village republics' of which Metcalfe wrote that he seems to have regarded as particularly important. Marx repeated a long passage from Metcalfe on the subject in a letter to Engels in 1853,[22] and later, in 1867, incorporated the substance of Metcalfe's account into Book I of *Capital*.[23] At a later period of his life, however, Marx became acquainted with some work on the subject by the Russian sociologist M. M. Kovalevsky, and although he disagreed with Kovalevsky's conclusions which equated the Asiatic mode with feudalism,[24] he seems from then onwards to have omitted the Asiatic mode from his philosophy of economic history. Later Marxist writers dropped all reference to the Asiatic mode and thus avoided committing themselves to the fallacy that Indian rural society was, when left to itself, unchanging. As the Indian Marxist historian D. D. Kosambi put it in 1956, 'What Marx himself said about India cannot be taken as it stands.'[25]

Modern sociological studies of Indian rural life present a rather different picture from that which is enshrined in the idea of primitive self-sufficient republic. 'An Indian village typically is hardly a republic; it has certainly changed from time to time; and it clearly was not and is not self-sufficient.'[26] Marriage affiliations; the need for specialist services even at a rural level; travel to market; religious pilgrimage; these and other regular features of Indian rural life have always entailed a good deal of travel between the village and the surrounding region; they entail, also, the intersection of village boundaries by those of kinship, occupation, religious cult-adherence, and so on. Change, moreover, although it might be slow and, for long periods, imperceptible, was nevertheless as real a feature of traditional Indian village life as of any other rural society.[27]

It appears, therefore, that Marx's sources led him into making an incorrect analysis of Indian society and Hindu religion. He believed that Hindu religion and despotic rule were largely independent of each other, both resting alike on the village community and the Asiatic mode of production. He did not conceive the possibility that in India, as in Europe, religion could be a means of social control, used by political rulers and other élite classes in their own interests. Yet this, as we shall see, was in fact the case throughout much of India's history. Marx, on the basis of inadequate data, saw the inter-relationship of religion, the state, and socio-economic realities in India as quite different from the inter-relationship he had discovered in the case of Prussia where the state was protecting and upholding a religion which might otherwise have withered away. Hindu religion, according to Marx, was a primitive worship of Nature and reflected man's non-rational attitude to Nature. In his view, the traditional character of Indian village life guaranteed the continuance of Hindu religion without need of state protection. For only when the basic pattern of village communities was destroyed would Hindu religion begin to decay. Only then would it need a Hindu state's protection. But the very factor which was now about to dissolve the village communities, namely, British rule and especially British free trade, would not only guarantee the inability of Hindu power to revive Hindu religion but would also be the least likely itself to protect that religion. For Marx noted in 1857 that whereas, formerly, the British had avoided tampering with native religion in India, more recently under Disraeli a new principle had been introduced: in order to destroy Indian nationality there had been deliberate 'tampering with the religion of the people'.[28]

Hindu religion, in Marx's view, was doomed to die in the foreseeable future when the village communities had been dissolved and disappeared in 'the only *social* revolution ever heard of in Asia'.[29] That Marx was mistaken in this view (as we shall see that he was) may be due, to some extent, to the sources he relied so heavily upon, and the idealised view of Indian rural life which they conveyed. It was also due partly to the incomplete, hurried and disrupted nature of Marx's study of India. After all this was a subject on the periphery of his horizons; more immediate concerns in Europe inevitably captured his attention and apart from the two brief excursions which he made into the study of Indian society under the impulsion of immediate events, in 1853 and 1857, and some even slighter glances at other Asian societies, he remained, as Shlomo Avineri has said, a European-oriented thinker. Whether Avineri is justified in his further comment in this connection may be doubted however. For he concludes that Marx's 'insights into Indian and Chinese society could never be reconciled with his general philosophy of history, which remained – like Hegel's – determined by the European experience and the Western historical consciousness'.[30]

There are good grounds for claiming that if Marx had had access to the kind of sources which are now available for the study of Indian society, he would have been able to demonstrate a large extent of agreement between the role of ecclesiastical religion in Germany in the 1840s and the role of the Brāhmans in religion in India, in the nineteenth century as well as in many preceding centuries. There are greater possibilities for using Marx's basic model of the social relationship between religion and economic interests in the Indian case than has generally been supposed. Had Marx had access to more adequate sources of information he would certainly have been able to find examples of situations in Indian history where religion, especially Brāhmanical religion, had played a role very similar to that which state Protestantism had played in Europe.

Another aspect of this subject which Marx somewhat surprisingly passed over in silence, and which greater familiarity with Indian history would have enabled him to assess more realistically, is the role of Muslims in Indian religion and society. He appears to have assumed too simplistically that the Muslims of India had been 'Hinduised' to such an extent that their social organisation and culture had retained no distinctive features which could affect the general social and cultural situation independently of Hindu social formations. On such a view of Muslim life in India as Marx appears to have taken, the extent of the actual and very considerable conversions to Islam from among the native population is inexplicable.

The first of these two aspects of the incompleteness of Marx's account, namely, his inadequate perception of the realities of Hindu religion and society, will be dealt with in greater detail in chapter 8.[31]

For Marx, religious change *followed* economic and social change but never inaugurated it. The type of religion which was adhered to in any given society was the type appropriate to that society and economy. Folk religion such as that of India was associated with societies having a simple structure and economy, just as Protestantism was the appropriate form of religion for a bourgeois–capitalist society. The type of religion present was significant, therefore, as an indication of the present state of the society, but had no significance as a pointer to what social or economic changes might or might not occur in the future. The theory that a religion can, by its own ideology and organisation, inhibit economic development – as for example Islam is sometimes alleged to have done – would not have been countenanced by Marx. For in the Marxian view religious ideas and practices do not *effect* anything in the social and economic sphere; they are simply the *reflection* of social and economic realities.

However, even by Marx's criteria the study of religion can be sociologically profitable, if only for the clues it provides about the less superficially obvious aspects of social and economic realities. To put the matter at its most pointed: if Marx had been equipped to examine village religion in India more clearly he might have been alerted to certain features of rural Indian economic life which he seems to have missed. Certainly the sociologist today, whether his perspective is Marxian or not, can profit from the careful scrutiny of religion in rural India which is becoming increasingly possible, whether his concern is with the recent past or with the present. One clue of this sort is found in the political, economic and social role of the high castes, particularly the Brāhman, and on this much fuller data are available today than Marx had at his disposal.

However, before this aspect of the sociology of Indian religion is considered more fully in an attempt to see what Marx, from his characteristic stance, could have made of this fuller evidence, another possibly Marxian analysis of Indian religion has to be considered, namely, the work of Max Weber. For Weber came to the study of Indian religion half a century later than Marx. Much had been learnt in Europe about India in those intervening fifty years. Weber's work on Indian religion [32] gives ample evidence of this. If, therefore, Weber's sociology was as close in its general perspective to that of Marx as has sometimes been claimed, if 'the critical assessment of the mode of life stimulated in capitalism is quite remarkably similar in the writings of each author',[33] and if they both regard religion's destiny in modern societies in much the same way, then, with the added advantage of a fifty years' increment in resources and understanding, Weber's sociology of Indian religion might be expected to make up something of what was lacking in Marx's.

NOTES

1. David McLellan, *Karl Marx. His Life and Thought* (1976), p. 227.
2. 'The India Bill', *NYDT* (9 June 1853).
3. E. Hobsbawm, *Pre-capitalist Economic Formations* (1964), p. 22.
4. Ibid., p. 26.
5. S. Avineri, *Karl Marx on Colonialism and Modernization* (1968), p. 26.

6. V. G. Kiernan, *Marxism and Imperialism* (1974), p. 168.

7. 'British Rule in India', *NYDT* (25 June 1853).

8. Ibid.

9. Ibid.

10. Marx and Engels, *On Colonialism* (1974 edn), p. 357.

11. 'The Indian Revolt', *NYDT* (16 September 1857).

12. 'Investigation of Torture in India', *NYDT* (17 September 1857).

13. Letter to Engels (14 June 1853), *On Colonialism* (1974), p. 315; see also letter to N. F. Danielson (19 Feb. 1881), ibid., p. 349.

14. 'The British Army in India', *NYDT* (26 June 1858).

15. 'The Future Result of British Rule in India', *NYDT* (8 August 1853).

16. See G. Campbell, *Modern India: A Sketch of the System of Civil Government* (London, 1852), pp. 84 – 5 for example.

17. K. A. Witlfogel, *Oriental Despotism* (1957), p. 372ff.

18. 'The British Rule in India', *NYDT* (25 June 1853).

19. Ibid.

20. *Capital*, Bk. I, ch. 1, pp. 79 – 81. See K. Marx and F. Engels, *On Religion*, pp. 120f; and Karl Marx, *Capital*, vol. I (Penguin Books, 1976), pp. 172 – 3.

21. For other sources used by Marx see Hobsbawm, p. 22, n. 2.

22. Marx to Engels (London, 14 June 1853). *On Colonialism*, p. 313f.

23. See Karl Marx, *Selected Writings in Sociology and Social Philosophy*, ed. by T. B. Bottomore and Maximilian Rubel (Pelican Books, 1963), p. 122f.

24. See Hobsbawm, p. 58.

25. D. D. Kosambi, *An Introduction to the Study of Indian History* (1956), pp. 11 – 12; see also M. N. Srinivas and A. M. Shah, 'The Myth of the Self-sufficiency of the Indian Village', *The Economic Weekly*, vol. 12.

26. David G. Mandelbaum, *Society in India* (Indian edn, 1970), p. 328.

27. See Mandelbaum, pp. 425 – 659; also M. Singer and B. S. Cohn (eds), *Structure and Change in Indian Society* (1968); Ramkrishna Mukherjee, *The Sociologist and Social Change in India Today* (1965), ch. seven: 'Orientation for Depth Analysis: Role of Tradition in Social Change'.

28. 'The Indian Question', *NYDT* (14 August 1857).

29. See above, note 18.

30. Avineri, p. 27f.

31. The second, a rounding out of Marx's critique of religion as it applies to Islam in south Asia, is too large an undertaking to be included here and demands a separate book if it is to be treated adequately.

32. *The Religion of India: the Sociology of Hinduism and Buddhism*, trans. and ed. by Hans. H. Gerth and Don Martindale (1958).

33.   Anthony Giddens, *Capitalism and Modern Social Theory* (1971), p. 215.

6 Weber and Indian Religion

(i) *Is Weber's perspective Marxian?*

WEBER'S book, *The Religion of India*, is one of the few, and certainly one of the earliest, full-length accounts of Indian religion produced by a sociologist. What is more, Weber's work has been regarded by some social scientists as having a strongly Marxist affinity. For example, Joseph Schumpeter's assessment of Weber has been frequently quoted: 'The whole of Max Weber's facts and arguments [in his sociology of religion] fits perfectly into Marx's system'.[1] Irving Zeitlin takes the view that Weber 'generalised and revised Marx's method', and argues that Weber was not refuting Marx, and that to say, as Talcott Parsons has, that after an early contact with the Marxian position Weber 'soon recoiled from this, becoming convinced of the indispensability of an important role of "ideas" in the explanation of great historical processes' is quite incorrect.[2]

First it will be necessary to look briefly at Weber's personal background; then to consider the method and main argument of *The Religion of India*; and finally to evaluate these in terms of the distinction which has been made already between, broadly, an idealist, theological perspective and one that is materialist and non-theological.

(ii) *Personal background*

Max Weber was born on 21 April 1864. His father was a lawyer and a magistrate in the town of Erfurt, and had himself grown up in a comfortable home whose atmosphere was that of 'the Protestant orthodoxy prevalent in Westphalia'. Max's grandfather had also been a 'bourgeois notable', the co-founder of a large firm dealing in linen, and himself a good representative of what his grandson was later to write about as the 'spirit' of capitalism.[3] Max's mother Helene and his maternal grandmother were also 'profoundly religious but were far more liberal and had no dogmatic ties'.[4] Max was the first child; seven more were to follow, but at the time of his birth his mother Helene was unable to breastfeed him. The feeding of the infant was therefore entrusted to a wet nurse, 'the wife of a Social Democratic carpenter', relates Marianne Weber; she adds that 'when later his social and democratic views developed in opposition to the political heritage of his ancestors, the family used to joke that "Max drank in his political views with his nurse's milk" '.[5]

At Heidelberg University Max Weber studied jurisprudence and, in addition, history, economics and philosophy. After a year's voluntary military service at Strasbourg from 1883 – 4 he resumed his life as a student, this time at the University of Berlin.

It is clear that Weber had a moral attachment to the values of Protestantism, even though he had intellectual difficulties about its doctrines. The letter which he wrote to his younger brother Alfred at the time of the latter's confirmation at the age of sixteen (Max was then aged twenty), shows a solemn respect even for the doctrines which he himself found it difficult to hold. He was writing 'a few words as a brother and a Christian' to one who was already 'familiar with the doctrines of Christianity as they have been believed and observed in our church from time immemorial'; their significance, he said, 'differs for different people' and each person 'attempts to solve in his own way the great riddles that this religion poses'. Commitment to Christianity is quite clear in this epistle of Weber's:

> I believe the greatness of the Christian religion lies in the very fact that it is available in equal measures to every person. . . . It is one of the chief foundations on which everything great in our time rests. The nations that have come into being, all the great deeds they have performed, the great laws and regulations they have recorded, even science and all great ideas of mankind have developed primarily under the influence of Christianity. . . .

There is more in the same strain, and it is quite clear where Weber's moral commitment was.[6]

The same attitude underlies the collaboration of Weber later on with Friedrich Naumann, a chaplain to a mission in Frankfurt-am-Main and 'leader of the younger members of the Christian-Social movement', who 'hoped that Marxism would be conquered from within by a living and developing Christianity', and that 'it would be possible to place alongside the Social Democratic Workers' Movement an equally well prepared Christian movement that would not be tied down by Marxism and international connections'.[7] Weber met Naumann at an Evangelical-Social congress, and his wife records that their 'acquaintance soon blossomed into friendship'.[8] She adds that gradually the two forged common political and social aims: 'The goal of both men's political action was a fatherland organised along the lines of a power state with a growing, hard-working population whose complete political maturity would enable it both to protect its own rights and to share in the responsibility for the fate of the nation.'[9]

It is not necessary to retail further evidence of this kind. Weber himself, in the opening pages of *The Protestant Ethic and the Spirit of Capitalism*, makes very clear his position when he wrote that essay in 1903 at the age of thirty-nine; his admiration for Christianity, and for Protestantism in particular, had not diminished. The theme of the Introduction is that Christian civilisation has been responsible for the fullest and finest developments of every kind in human life: 'the full development of a systematic theology', jurisprudence, art, music, architecture, science, government, and above all, 'the most fateful force in our modern life, capitalism'. The reason Weber suggests for all this, and particularly for the very special and much superior form of capitalist economy produced in Europe, is 'the specific and peculiar rationalism of Western culture'.[10] The ultimate credit for this, as the rest of the essay is intended to show, lies within Protestantism.

Bryan Turner has shown that Weber's religious attitude and the tensions and ambiguities of his personal life, particularly his courtship of Emmy Baumgartner and then his marriage to Marianne, left him with a feeling of guilt which aggravated the difficulties he already had in his sexual life and probably contributed to the failure to consummate his marriage. He 'lived out the moral content of the Protestant Ethic', and in every sense; 'he was morally and emotionally committed to the values of Pro-testantism.'[12] Marx's attitude to religion was completely impersonal; his attachment and marriage to Jenny was happy, long and very fruitful, and 'his personal life was not complicated by the anxieties of guilt'. His atheism was critical, but not militant. In short, Turner concludes, 'Marx's sociology is atheist and critical; Weber's sociology is agnostic and judgmental.'[13] One might add that the less agnostic Weber became (and I am inclined to rate his agnosticism lower than Bryan Turner does) the more theologically judgemental he became. In a refined fashion it is this that shows especially in his sociology of the world religions.

(iii) *Weber's sociology of religion*

Weber claimed to have identified the ideological factor which had contributed to the rise of capitalist industrialism, namely, 'the spirit of capitalism'; and this originated, Weber asserted, in the Protestant ethic. More particularly it was to be identified in the spirit and lifestyle of those Protestants who adhered to late forms of Calvinistic belief such as the Westminster Confession of 1647, and most of all among certain religious sects such as the Quakers and others whose beliefs prevented their members from entering government service, military service, or the legal profession, so that the possibilities of choice of an occupation were narrowed towards some kind of business enterprise. These sects were, moreover, of a kind which disposed their members to an ascetic style of life in which hard work was combined with the absolute minimum of pleasure of any kind, so that the profits of their enterprise could not be expended in personal enjoyment or aesthetic pursuits, the arts or the theatre and so on, but had to be ploughed back into the business, thus continually enlarging the capital invested. It was on the basis of this finding that Weber then set out to discover why the 'spirit of capitalism' had not emerged from other cultures, particularly that of Judaism and also, in Asia, the cultures of China and India.

Weber was the first major scholar in modern times to engage in the comparative study of religion over so wide an area. He went farther afield and crossed more frontiers in search of his data than any one scholar in the field of religion before him, and possibly since. From his early studies of southern-European economic and cultural history he turned his attention to Protestantism in Germany. Then, in search of comparative data for his study of the growth of bureaucratic capitalism, he turned to China, Japan, India and south-east Asia, Palestine and to the Islamic world. He was concerned with a two-way interaction. His own interests were ultimately political, as a quotation from his inaugural lecture at Freiberg illustrates: 'In the last analysis, the processes of economic development are struggles for power. Our ultimate yardstick of values is "reasons of state", and this is also the yardstick for our economic reflections. . . .'[14] In this connection Gerth and Mills have suggested that Weber's role in relation to Marx was 'to "round out" Marx's economic materialism by a political and military materialism. The Weberian approach to political structures closely parallels the Marxian approach to economic structures.'[15] At the end of *The Protestant Ethic and the Spirit of Capitalism*, Weber points out that in that essay he has dealt with only one aspect of the connection between religion and capitalism; he has traced how, in his view, capitalism was an indirect consequence of the Protestant ethic. But then he adds, 'It would also further be necessary to investigate how Protestant asceticism was in turn influenced in its development and in its character by the totality of social conditions, especially economic.'[16] What really constitutes his interest in religious ideas is revealed in his essay on the 'Social Psychology of the World Religions'. He states his point of view quite unambiguously: that not ideas alone 'but material and ideal interests directly govern men's conduct'. The mode of operation of ideal interests is described by Weber as that of triggering off one or other possible courses of economic and political activity; '. . . very frequently the "world-images" that have been created by "ideas" have, like signalmen, determined the tracks along which action has been pushed by the dynamic of interest'.[17] That is to say, religious ideas do not lay down the tracks along which the economic activities of the group concerned are to go, they merely act as the lever which sets economic activity off along one or other of the possible routes. It is clear from Weber's comparative studies that he is saying, in effect, one signalman will send the train along this track, but if another signalman happens to be on duty he will send it along the other. One religious ethic will have the effect of switching economic activity towards industrial capitalism, whereas another will keep it rolling along in the countryside, in a peasant economy. From the point of view of planners who are concerned with economic development, Indian religion might seem to be blameworthy for its apparently large part in retarding economic progress, if Weber's view is correct. But in that view of the matter it would be blame wrongly bestowed.

(iv) *The religion of India*

One of the facts about India that everyone knows is that it is largely Hindu. This is so in the sense that in the 1971 Census about 84 per cent of the population of the Republic were returned as Hindu, 10 per cent Muslim; the remaining 6 per cent were people of some four or five other faiths, or none at all. Again everyone knows that India is not only predominantly Hindu but also that the Republic of India is, in comparison with the USA or the EEC, a poor country; more euphemistically an under-developed or developing country.[18] So well have the promoters of international private charity in the West done their work that the image of India, seen by the majority of people here, is that of a perpetually starving mass of weak, sickly and superstitious villagers. It is hardly to be expected that at least some of the citizens of the West will avoid making the correlation which it seems to them is just asking to be made, between Indian religion and culture and this horrific widespread poverty. It has, in fact, been done fairly frequently. Max Weber was not above reproach in this respect and may in recent years, since his works have become more widely known among English readers, have been partly responsible for maintaining this point of view.

It is important to make clear that Weber only wrote *about* India, and that he never visited the subcontinent. It is clear from the evidence of his writings that he did not know India at first-hand. Weber certainly travelled widely; he visited Italy, Holland, Belgium, Switzerland, Scotland, and quite a number of places in the USA. He crossed many international frontiers, but not apparently those of India. So far as I know he belongs to the glorious company of those who have written with great confidence about India, but have never lived there. A list of their names would include a number of famous writers besides Max Weber, and it may be argued that these all wrote more cogently about India precisely because they had never experienced India at first-hand, for they were not emotionally involved one way or the other. When one considers some of the bitter works which have been penned from Bombay hotel bedrooms by men whose bowels were suffering from the first, possibly injudicious encounter with Indian life, one is inclined to think that there is perhaps something to be said for this view: *they* would have written more reasonably had they stayed at home. A former colleague of mine used to hold it to be a fallacy that travel broadens a student's mind. Instead of making uncomfortable journeys to far-off places, he argued, students would be much more profitably employed exploring the ample contents of the University Library.

Certainly this was very much more Max Weber's method of collecting data, traveller though indeed he was for other reasons. Edwardian India was not for him the magnet which the modern Republic of India has since become for large numbers of his package-touring fellow-countrymen. On the other hand he certainly appears to have ransacked the libraries in search of authoritative and up-to-date accounts of Indian religion and society. An interesting exercise for the Indologist or the historian of modern India now would be to think back to the year 1911 or just before, when Weber was preparing to write his long essay, *Hinduismus und Buddhismus*,[19] and to compile a list of the important works which were available at that time, and which would need to be taken into account by anyone embarking on such an essay. His list would probably tally fairly closely with what Weber himself discloses concerning his sources, in the course of his very full footnotes. Inevitably, since British anthropologists, administrators and orientalists had the easiest access to the field, much of the relevant literature was in English, and of this Weber made full use, including the extensive descriptive material published as part of the Report on the Census of India in 1911, which must have become available to him while he was writing. He relied fairly heavily, too, on the work of German Indologists. But what is significant about Weber's bibliography, and distinguishes it sharply from the kind of bibliography one would compile today as the basis for an account of contemporary Indian religion and society, is that his sources are almost all Western. He mentions two or three early twentieth-century Indian authors who wrote in English,[20] but on the whole his information comes to him through Western eyes and ears. This said, it is only doing Weber the barest justice to record the admiration which the extent of his knowledge of Indian culture can still evoke sixty years later.

Although Weber may not have visited India in person, he is certainly known in that country today, at any rate among Indian social scientists. A chapter could be devoted entirely to the subject of Max Weber in India in the sense of the reception Weber's work has had among Indian scholars, especially since English translations of his work began to appear more rapidly after the Second World War. Aldous Huxley, in an essay entitled 'Wordsworth in the tropics', points out that Wordsworth's poetry reflected the English countryside for the very good reason that that was the countryside he knew, mild and moderate. But to quote Huxley, 'Nature, under a vertical sun and nourished by equatorial rains, is not at all that chaste, mild deity who presides over the *Gemütlichkeit*, the prettiness, the cosy sublimities of the Lake District.' Huxley then goes on to explore the idea of how very different Wordsworth's poetry might have been had he visited the jungles of Borneo or Malaya. I am concerned to imagine the difference it might have made to Weber and his treatment of Indian religion, had he visited India. After all Wordsworth did not claim to be writing about the tropics. Weber did claim to be writing about India, and he might have written a rather different account of the place of religion in the life of modern India if he had, as a mature scholar, spent the requisite year or two which a social scientist would today be required to spend in his research area.

Such a period of field-work might have led Weber to modify some of his conclusions regarding the responsibility of Indian religious ideas and practices for what he sees as the failure of India to develop a bureaucratic capitalism of the kind which had developed in Europe. His negative conclusions regarding the Indian case is arrived at in the context of a discussion of the role in Indian life of the *guru*, that is, the spiritual master or personal religious adviser. Weber draws attention to what he calls 'the power of mystagogues and magicians'[21] with their personal charismatic qualities, which are, he points out with care, of a quite irrational kind. Rationality or its absence was, according to Weber, an important indicator of the presence or absence of the kind of ethic which would be likely to favour the development of capitalism, so he was ceaselessly on the look-out for it in all the societies he studied.

(v) *Hindus and the spirit of capitalism*

The growth of the influence of the *gurus* in Indian society Weber sees as a consequence of the foreign domination of India by Islam, during the period of Mughal rule. Earlier, he says, under Hindu kings, such charismatic sectarian leaders were kept firmly in check by the established clergy, the brāhmans, acting with royal support and approval. But the military conquest and political domination of India by Muslims 'shattered the political power of the distinguished (that is, high-ranking) Hindu castes, which gave the development of *guru*-power free reign, permitting it to grow to grotesque heights'.[22] The growth of such irrational sectarian groups, says Weber, 'hindered the rationalisation of life-conduct throughout. It is quite evident that no community dominated by inner powers of this sort could out of its substance arrive at the "Spirit of capitalism".' It was, he adds, 'even unable to take over the economic and technically finished form [that is, of capitalism] as an artefact, as occurred in Japan'.[23]

   The factor responsible for what Weber believed to be India's economic backwardness was *not* identified by him as Hinduism. For Hinduism is simply a word of Anglo-German manufacture, with no single clear referent in the Indian situation. True Weber used the word *Hinduismus* in the title of his essay, but he did not employ it as a concept to be used in the analysis of the Indian socio-economic situation. For the word 'Hinduism', as the author of the Report on the 1911 Census of India emphasises, covers far too wide a range of meanings to be acceptable as a tool of demographic or any other analysis. What is called 'Hinduism', he declares, is of a highly heterogeneous nature, 'a complex congeries of creeds and doctrines'.[24] A

Census Report of 1881 had made the same point: the word Hinduism lumps together everything in Indian culture from the surviving forms of Aryan theistic belief to the demon-worship of Tinnevelly.[25] It has, in fact, about the same heuristic value as the term Europeanism would have if there were such a term to cover the range of ideologies and practices from Teutonic mythology and the mother-goddess cults of southern Europe, through Papacy and Puritanism to Pentecostalism and Marxism. Hinduism similarly has a geographical reference; it refers to the whole indigenous culture of the subcontinent.

What Weber identified, more precisely, as the cause of India's failure to win the modernisation race and develop some form of industrial capitalism was what he called the salvation religions or cults. India, like Europe, has developed its own indigenous forms of religious belief centring round the notion of salvation by divine grace through faith. These, said Weber, in India entailed a devaluation of the world and an absolute flight from the world. Whatever the means adopted for reaching the holy goal of salvation, all these Indian cults alike were characterised, he says, by irrationality. 'Either they were of an orgiastic character and linked quite immediately in anti-rational manner to the course of each alien life in methodology, or they were indeed rational in method but irrational in goal.'[26] Venturing a little way into the realm of prediction, Weber quotes with apparent approval and concurrence the view of certain English authorities that such industrialism as has been developed in India under British rule would not long survive if the enlightened and reasonable rule of the British were removed and India were to become independent.[27]

As it has turned out, the economic development of the Republic of India has been conspicuously more rapid since independence was achieved. Any number of economic reports are available for the periods before and after 1947. Some of these have been summarised recently by Angus Maddison, formerly head of the economics division of the OEEC. The real national income of India, says Maddison, has grown by 3.3 per cent per year since 1948, and *per capita* income has also grown each year since independence, compared 'with a more or less stagnant level from 1900 to 1946', that is, under British rule. 'India's post-war economic growth is much more than it was under colonial rule', he comments, 'and is a legitimate source of national pride.'[28] During more recent years, in the period from 1960 to 1965, national income grew by an average of about 4.7 per cent per annum.[29] This was in spite of a growth of population which has been a drag on the economy, and the need to maintain large armed forces. From 1965 to 1967 India's economic progress was temporarily halted by two extremely bad years of drought and the war with China. But since 1968 progress has been continued. This progress has been partly due to improvements in the agricultural sector, but also in a large measure to the deliberate policy of industrialisation which has been followed in the series of India's Five Year Plans, the first of which began in 1951. India today, thirty-two years after independence, has her own heavy iron and steel industries, motor-car industry, a well-developed electronics industry, an advanced nuclear power programme, jet-aircraft industry and so on. The intention of the central government is that, within the foreseeable future, India will be independent of foreign economic aid.

Where, then, did Max Weber go wrong? What has become of his eternally medieval India whose life would always be dominated, vitiated and impeded by irrational sects and salvation religions? Initially the answer is this: Indian society never was *dominated* by irrational mystical sects at any period, either in Weber's time or before, although Bengal certainly came fairly near to that condition in the latter period of Mughal rule in the eighteenth century. But we must look at this in more detail.

(vi) *This-worldly concerns in village religion*

Weber himself acknowledged that the vast mass of the people of India, as he said, 'knew nothing about (the idea of) salvation, or *moksha*. They hardly knew the expression, let alone its meaning. Except for short periods it must always have been so.'[30] The interests of the mass of the people are quite simply this-worldly, he acknowledged.[31] The Hindu sects, wrote Weber, do not address themselves to the masses, and on a basis of membership they comprise scarcely more than 5 per cent of the people.[32] His statistics are from the 1911 Census of India.

What is thus accurately perceived by Weber is that the mass of Indian people, the peasants who make up about 75 per cent of the population, are predominantly secular in their aims, attitudes and styles of life. True they engage fairly regularly in practices which at first sight appear to have some connection with other-worldiness, or the sacred, or forms of salvation-religion. But when these cultic practices of Indian village life are examined more closely, they are found to have an overwhelmingly this-worldly reference. Reports made by various observers, who have from time to time looked closely and carefully at village life in India, present a remarkable unanimity on this point. From Lal Bihari Dey's minutely detailed account of Bengal life in the 1830s to the village survey monographs forming part of the Report on the 1961 Census of India, and the many independent village surveys made by Indian social anthropologists in the 1960s, there is a continuing line of evidence of the immediate, this-worldly concerns which define the horizon of the mass of Indian peasants, and which constitute a thorough-going secularism.

Cultic practices do give this secularism, however, a religious character. In village temple, or wayside shrine beneath some large and ancient tree, the countryman uses various traditional rituals; what he seeks is a variety of mundane boons. Characteristic of many others is the list, provided by a Bengal anthropologist, of the stated intentions for which offerings were made at four village temples in Midnapur, West Bengal, over a period of six months from October 1956 to March 1957.[33] They are as follows in order of frequency of cases: for the cure of disease; for acknowledgement of cure of disease; for good health; for the birth of a child; for prosperity in trade; for employment; for abundant crops; for securing property; for cure of cattle disease; for progress in education; for success in a law-suit; for domestic peace; for victory in a football match; for success in local amateur dramatics; for making a good match in marriage. In similar vein those who were engaged in the village surveys made in connection with the 1961 Census mention, in monograph after monograph, the purposes for which villagers offer worship to the local goddesses, such as Śitala, or Chandī, or Manasā: for immunity to smallpox and cholera (over which the goddess Śitala is held to be the controlling power), for protection against wild animals (Chandī); for protection against snake-bite (Manasā); or for the birth of a child; the recovery of a sick child, and so on.[34]

The important point to notice is that these intentions are almost entirely this-worldly and secular. They could be pursued by alternative modern methods. The villager's chief concern is to use the most efficacious means of gaining his ends. Given a change of circumstances, these ends could be sought in other ways – through smallpox vaccination or anti-snake serum, through a labour exchange or a marriage bureau, through the use of fertility pills or crop fertilisers – and those other ways *might* be found to be more effective than folk rituals. What is certainly significant is that in those districts of West Bengal which are nearest to Calcutta, districts where modernisation has made more rapid progress, the new rituals *are* replacing the old; vaccination is being accepted and the goddess of smallpox is receiving correspondingly fewer oblations.

Salvation-religions, on the other hand, or sects which promise some other-worldly or supramundane benefits are of very limited extent in terms of the percentage of the population which adheres to them. Max

Weber was aware of this: he noted that in 1911 only 5 per cent of the people did so. It was this kind of minority, however, which seems always to have caught the attention of Western observers. It is the Maharishis, the jet-set swamia, the yogins, the most spectacularly ascetic sadhus standing for twenty years on one leg, the emotional fervour of the Baishnabs singing their way to salvation, these and other similar spiritual types which have fascinated, captivated, horrified or repelled Europeans for several centuries now. Ever since the seventeenth century, when the northern-European nations discovered this rich source of goods and material profit known to them as India, they have loved to dwell on the spirituality of India. It is remarkable how often someone in the West who is looking for a reference level of other-worldly spirituality takes India as the example.

But the real situation, certainly in 1911, as the somewhat more perceptive, or more honest, author of the Census Report saw, was that, as he wrote, 'the tendency of the people is to classify their neighbours not according to their beliefs, but according to their social status and manner of living. No one is interested in what his neighbour believes. . . .' In another place in the Report one finds this observation: 'Of the great mass of Hindus only a relatively small minority belong definitely to special sects, and still fewer have any idea that their particular cult differentiates them in any way from other Hindus.'[35] A Bengali scholar and writer of the period comments, 'The bulk of the Hindus are not sectaries. Though the [religious] sects write much and make the most noise, they are only a small minority.'[36]

Max Weber recognised this, of course, but he assumed that the 5 per cent who were religiously concerned were influential. 'The sects and their redemption religiosity', he wrote, 'were and are an opportunity for the mainly middle strata, advised by intellectuals, to achieve salvation through the power of contemplation'. In this way, Weber argued, philosophical or theological sects with their promises of other-worldly salvation did have 'most enduring indirect influence on the conduct of the masses'.[37]

It is at this point that one may suspect there would have been a substantial difference in Weber's too easy assumptions concerning the way minority religious ideas influenced the attitudes and life-styles of the masses had he been closely in touch with events in India between, say, 1905 and 1912 when he was writing. It is at this point in his argument that Weber's lack of familiarity with the Indian situation and his heavy reliance on Western official and semi-official writers become serious disadvantages, and result in distortion. For he had, in effect, no alternative but to project on to Indian society and culture certain postulated connections between religious ideas, values, and behaviour, without testing them by empirical study. As Milton Singer has pointed out, there is in Weber's theory about Indian religion and its effects a serious failure 'to specify conditions and magnitudes under which the conclusions are valid'. One needs to know 'how many ascetics would retard [economic] growth by how much and under what conditions'.[38]

This is a failure which has, unhappily, characterised the comparative study of religion in more cases than this. Impressionistic accounts have been accepted as established findings, and too often there has been no attempt to quantify just where quantification would have been appropriate. This is connected with the failure in comparative religion to test hypothesis by field research. In the case of Weber's study there were two related areas which required empirical investigation. One was the real extent of adherence to different salvation cults – in terms of numbers of adherents – in order to provide a more refined analysis of what the Census of India Report could offer in fairly crude terms. The other was a study of the degree of facility with which salvation cults, and religious ideas associated with such cults, were really being communicated to the large majority of the population who did *not* adhere to these cults. This is perhaps asking too much in the way of sophisticated field research in the year 1911. It would, however, certainly not be justifiable now for the comparative study of religion to proceed in a spirit of blithe disregard of such requirements.

Let us suppose that Weber had found it possible to visit India sometime between 1905 and 1911. Let us suppose that he would have made for that part of India where the action was in those years, namely Bengal. It was in 1911 that Calcutta ceased to be the capital of the British-Indian Empire and the whole machinery of central government was transferred to a safer location, namely Delhi. The reasons why British administrators decided to make the move are relevant to our subject and to Weber's analysis of the Indian tradition.

(vii) *The Growth of middle-class religion and nationalism*

The middle stratum of Indian society, of which Weber writes, was particularly prominent in Bengal. The emergence of this middle class was to some extent the consequence of British policy with regard to land tenure laid down in the Permanent Settlement of 1793. A new class of *zamindars*, or landowners, had emerged, many of whom became absentee landlords living in Calcutta and the adjacent towns on the Hooghly river. During the nineteenth century they established themselves in education and certain administrative occupations. During the earlier decades of the nineteenth century some of the members of this class had been actively concerned with religious reform movements, notably the Brahmo Samaj. But even this well-publicised organisation had a relatively narrow social base and was supported by only a portion even of the middle class. In the last quarter of the nineteenth century educated Indians were giving their most enthusiastic support to those religious movements which were also strongly *nationalistic* in character. These movements were in large measure a reaction to the contemptuous attitudes towards Hindu culture adopted by some British officials, and the thoroughly aggressive anti-Hindu propaganda put out by Christian missionaries. For a time, therefore, specifically Hindu organisations served as channels for a strongly running reactionary current of Indian patriotism. So strongly secular was the motivation underlying this resurgent Hindu spirit that even the sixteenth-century Bengali religious leader and mystic, Chaitanya, was represented as having been primarily a great social reformer and liberator. Such a view of Chaitanya may have been unwarranted, but nevertheless to Surendranath Banerjea, the leader of the Indian National Congress, this is how Chaitanya and other theistic-salvation leaders in Bengal's religious history were now being presented; they were, wrote Banerjea, men 'who have lived dedicated lives, consecrated to the service of their country or their God'.[39] God and country were and are very closely linked in Bengali tradition.

Eventually, however, the dominantly political concern could not be contained within the neo-Hindu religious organisations and broke out into newer channels, notably the Indian National Congress founded in 1885. A great new impetus was given to political activism throughout Bengal in 1905 by Lord Curzon's partition of the province into East and West Bengal.

Even some of those movements which continued under an avowedly religious label, such as the Ramakrishna Mission, founded in 1897 and led by Swami Vivekananda, had a strongly nationalistic orientation. In an account of Vivekananda's life, written by one of his disciples and entitled *Swami Vivekananda, Patriot-Prophet*, it is affirmed that 'Swamiji's sayings were the source of inspiration to young revolutionaries of Bengal, and outside, during the days [sic] between 1901 and 1916.'[40] This seems to be confirmed by the fact that when the police raided houses in Calcutta where student revolutionaries were living, a matter which was considered worth reporting by the police was that they had discovered books by Swami Vivekananda. However by the first decade of the twentieth century the focus of interest and activity for the middle class in Bengal, and, as a result of their influence, among many of the urban labouring and even peasant classes also, lay in those organisations which were overtly political and nationalistic in their aims. As one modern Indian political scientist has put it, 'the legacy of Hindu resurgence was invested in nationalism'.[41]

By about 1910, therefore, such contributions as the theistic salvation-cults of India were making to the pattern of Indian public life, were mainly those of assisting and strengthening the dominantly political trend of nationalist activity. The religious cults do not appear to have been influential in encouraging any transcendentalist flight from this world and its affairs, or any devaluation of worldly concerns and activities; far from it. If any of the religious cults of India *were* trying to turn man's attention away from worldly pursuits, in 1910 they were not having much success with the majority of the people. They may have succeeded with a small minority of men, but their influence was certainly not of the supervisory and directing kind which Max Weber assumed it to be. There were always some who found in the mystical cults an escape route from the hurly-burly and the dangers of the battle which engaged most men at that time, that is, the independence struggle. But to provide an escape route for the drop-out minority is a different function from the one Weber attributed to the mystical cults – that of determining the course of public economic and political development in India. One such escaper from the battle was Aurobindo Ghose who, in February 1910, threatened with imprisonment by the British for the second time, retired to a safe place beyond their reach, namely to the French colony of Pondicherry, there to found an *āśram* and to contemplate in peace the ultimate unity of all things while his fellow countrymen in Bengal continued the struggle for freedom for another thirty-seven years. Weber, in effect, was taking the exceptional case, such as that of Aurobindo, as though it were the norm.

So if Weber had been in India in the years immediately preceding 1911 his own account of the otherworldliness of the Hindu people might have been considerably modified. Moreover he was in possession of certain clues which he might have scrutinised more rigorously than he did. One of them was the existence of a tradition of Indian rationality.

Weber himself was aware that there was a strongly rational element in Hindu culture. The heart of this rational orientation to the world lay in the attitudes and concerns of the brāhmans. But Weber's remote view of India as it was in the first decade of the twentieth century prevented him from detecting how strong a part was still being played by brāhmanical culture, certainly strong in comparison with the devotional salvation cults. It was this Indian, largely brāhmanical genius in mathematics which centuries before had given Europe the system of numerals known here erroneously as Arabic numerals – so known because they were mediated to the West by Islamic civilisation. It was this system which, once received in Europe, made arithmetical calculation much easier than it had been by the Roman system of using letters to represent numbers. (Try, for example, multiplying MCMLXXIV by LVI and you will see what is meant.) The Indian mathematician Bhāskara wrote a treatise in mathematics in the third century BC, dealing with the concept *nirvāna*, or *śuñyā*, or zero. It was this zero concept in particular, so I understand, which made possible early Indian mathematics. The zero symbol is that which stands for the sum of opposites, the neutral point in which all positive and negative numbers are inherent; it is also the symbol by the addition of which all the prime numbers from 1 to 9 can be made to express a power of expansion, tenfold or one hundredfold or to the nth degree.[42]

The same rationality characterises Sanskrit language and grammar, that is, the language used by the brāhmans, and the basis of the languages of north, west and east India. The Sanskrit alphabet is rationally constructed and the order of the consonants is related to the positions of the various organs of speech, the throat, the palate, the tongue, teeth and lips, unlike the chaotic and largely unsystematic arrangement of stops and vowels, without rhyme or reason, which we call our alphabet. Brāhmanical religious discussion and enquiry is another manifestation of this same regard for rational method and argument. In fact the objection could be raised that Indian philosophers have made religion *too* rational. It could be maintained also that the popular notion of *karma*, that is, the law of moral retribution, is too coldly calculating and leaves no room in the universe for generosity or free grace. But those who object to Indian religion on these grounds are, in doing so, implicitly acknowledging the supreme place given in brāhmanical culture to reason and calculation.

It is not only this trait, the calculating mentality, which has made Indians successful entrepreneurs; there is, of course, also their energetic pursuit of the enterprises which they launch, their readiness to work hard for attainment of their goals, to work no less hard than Weber's Calvinistic Puritans. This readiness to devote time and energy to the building up of a business, whether it is a grocer's shop in a back street in Headingly, an import business in Kampala, an emporium in Singapore, or a textile mill in

Bombay, might perhaps to some extent be related to the generally pervading Indian tradition that self-denial and austerity of life are to be admired and encouraged.

So when the question of India's present relatively lowly position in the world's economic league tables is raised, the answer has to be looked for in the combination of a number of factors. Explanations recently put forward by Indian and foreign economists have taken into account a variety of clearly non-religious factors, such as systems of land tenure inherited from British rule, climate, the disproportionately large Indian defence budget, the economic state of affairs at the transition to independence in 1947, regional jealousies, linguistic divisions, and so on. The major reasons lie here rather than in the nature of India's religion, or in any cultural inferiority of her people, or any lack of energy or enterprising spirit.

There is, of course, one very prominent indicator that Indians are not outstandingly otherworldly, and that they are not culturally conditioned against economic enterprise, This has become very evident since Weber's lifetime and it seriously vitiates his predictions. I refer to the commercial achievements of Indians who have settled in countries outside India; in Burma, in Malaya, and in East Africa, for example.

In Burma, until they were expelled by the military ruler General Ne Win in the early 1960s, Indians had fully established themselves as a commercial community before the beginning of the Second World War. By 1939 Indians were the owners in Burma of seven engineering factories, and twenty-eight other kinds of factories making sugar, metalware, matches, chemicals, and so on.[43] Indian assets in terms of factory ownership in Rangoon, in 1940, amounted to the equivalent of $11\frac{1}{4}$ million pounds sterling. The capital city of Burma, 'Rangoon, was essentially an Indian city', writes N. R. Chakravarti, and anyone who knew Rangoon before the mid-1960s will have no difficulty in agreeing. It was 'essentially an Indian city where a very large majority of landlords were Indians, who owned practically all the multi-storied residential quarters, mercantile houses, villas, important shopping centres, theatres and cinemas'.[44] Rangoon, though the largest, was not the only city in Burma where Indian enterprise had been established. In many others such as Akyab, Moulmein, Bassein, Mandalay, Pegu, and Maymyo, it was Indian businessmen who ran most of the commercial and industrial concerns which were not in the hands of the British.

(viii) *The Swadeshi movement and Indian capitalism*

The various commercial enterprises and trading activities of Indians in Malaya and Singapore are the subject of a recent very comprehensive and detailed study by K. S. Sandhu. The situation there was very similar to that of Burma, except that in Malaya the Indian community was matched by a Chinese community of similar size, and in Malaya these two originally foreign communities were to some extent being accepted as permanent parts of the Malaysian state and economy, whereas the Indians were not so accepted in Burma. According to Sandhu, 'the conclusion of British rule in Malaya found the Indians in almost every walk of Malayan economic life, their economic hierarchy ranging from cabinet ministers and wealthy financiers to countryside bread-sellers and toddy-tappers.'[45]

These examples of Indian business enterprise, which included the kind of capitalism that Weber believed could not emerge in Indian society, were only just about to manifest themselves at the time when Weber was recording his negative conclusion. But from the point of view of Weber's verdict on India, the unkindest twist of fate was that in 1911 the first really notable large-scale example of all-Indian industrial capitalism, the Tata Iron & Steel Company, began production. This was, as it happened, a quite direct result of the nationalism which had developed such strength in India in the previous decade. J. N. Tata, the originator of the idea of an Indian iron and steel company, had had considerable experience of the cotton textile industry which by the opening years of the twentieth century was, however, passing through a period of depression. For some time he had been nurturing the idea of developing the production of iron and steel. He died in 1904, but the scheme was taken up and pursued by his son, Dorabji Tata. In 1906 rich resources of iron ore were discovered in Mayurbhanja, in Bihar, which the Maharaja was prepared to allow Tata to work in return for royalties on the ore. The capital needed for the construction of the plant was £1¾ million. A prospectus was issued by Tata in August 1907. Nationalist fervour was at its height and the leaders of the movement were urging all Indians to join in and support the Swadeshi movement – to support Indian-owned production of every kind and to boycott British goods. The result was that 'from early morning till late at night the Tata offices in Bombay were besieged by an eager crowd of native investors, old and young . . . at the end of three weeks the entire capital for the construction requirement was secured, every penny contributed by some 8000 Indians. . . .'[46] The construction of the plant was begun in 1909. In 1911, when Weber was writing his *Hinduismus und Buddhismus*, the first iron ore was being produced by an Indian company, a company which was from that year onward to continue to grow and prosper, aided by the immediate impetus created by the government's military requirements of iron and steel during the First World War. Jamshedpur, or Tatanagar, the town which grew up around the Tata iron and steel works, increased in size from 5700 in 1911 to over 57,000 in 1921.[47] By 1961 its population was about 300,000 and it is still growing rapidly as the centre of a complex of industries.

The Tata Company was joined in the field of industrial capitalism by the Birlas, another Indian family which had been engaged in commercial and trading activities. By the 1920s the conversion of these and other Indian business concerns into industrial companies was a notable feature of the economic scene in India, although it has to be remembered that this kind of development was held in check for two decades or so by British industrial interests, until the end of the Second World War and the achievement of Indian independence.

Certainly, then, it seems that Weber was mistaken in assuming that Indian culture was of such a kind that it would inhibit industrial development, and even prevent India from taking over Western technological skills as Japan had done. The root of his mistake was that in his analysis of the situation in the early twentieth century he gave far too large a place to Indian religious salvation cults. He believed these were the major inhibiting factors which had until 1911, so far as he could tell. prevented the emergence of an indigenous bureaucratic capitalism in India. On the other hand, knowing what we now know, it would be equally erroneous for us to assume that the growth of Indian capitalistic enterprise is attributable in any positive sense to some *Hindu* factor in the situation. The point being made is that 'Hindu' is simply not a significant category in this connection. It is not *qua* Hindu that Indians succeed in business; some of those early entrepreneurs were Indians, but not Hindus. The significant differential factor is found at the level of the sub-culture, that of the caste to which a man belongs. It was not all Hindus in Burma or Malaya who succeeded in building up businesses in those countries; the labouring castes remained as labourers. It was outstandingly the Chettyar caste, and one or two other social sub-groups of a similar kind, who were economically successful. The Chettyars are a banking and business caste. In India itself the successful entrepreneurs have also included, very prominently, men of the Jain and Parsi communities. A recent field study of the light engineering industry in Howrah, part of the Calcutta urban area, has shown that success in the building up of small engineering businesses in this area is almost entirely the prerogative of the Mahisya caste.[48] These are people who were formerly engaged in agriculture and have migrated to the metropolitan area, where the life-style of their caste has given them a greater freedom to engage in engineering work, and hence a great advantage over potential rivals of other castes in that area, potential rivals in so far as they were capable of rational planning, but whose styles of life inhibited them from working as engineers themselves in the early stages of building a business.

The study of the history of religion was for a long time in the hands of those who had an interest in magnifying religion's importance. As the Master of Balliol has recently written: the history of religion was only slowly and painfully taken out of the hands of theologians.[49] Because they held the religious dimension to be supremely *important* they tended to take the view that religious belief had actually been very influential in shaping the course of history: they over-estimated its power and under-estimated the force of economic and sociological factors even within their own institutions. On the other hand, those who held opposing views tended to go to the other extreme, exaggerating religion's ineffectiveness and impotence, and seeing it as simply epiphenomenal. In general Max Weber was somewhere in between the two, and we have noted that he recognised that *both* ideal *and* material interests govern human affairs.

(ix) *Weber's ultimately non-Marxian position*

This recognition does not by itself justify the conclusion that Weber's perspective was necessarily different from that of Marx. For the latter also recognised that ideas had a certain force in history, as Zeitlin and others have pointed out.[50] It seems that in the attempts which have been made to relate Weber to Marx there is some unresolved ambiguity. We have the evidence of Weber's wife, in her *Biography* (see note 3), that Max Weber, in connection with his work in sociology, 'expressed great admiration for Karl Marx's brilliant constructions and saw in the inquiry into the economic and technical causes of events an exceedingly fruitful, indeed, a specifically new heuristic principle that directed the quest for knowledge (*Erkenntnistrieb*) into entire areas previously unilluminated'.[51] Elsewhere she records that 'Weber suspected all political metaphysics [that is metaphysics pressed into service by the state for political ends] up to that time as a kind of mimicry by which the privileged classes protected themselves against a re-arrangement of the spheres of power. In this respect he shared Karl Marx's conception of the state and its ideology.'[52]

The objection has, however, been raised by some Marxist sociologists that Weber's analysis finally gives too important a role to religious ideas as causal factors. Lukács, for example, has complained that Weber's sociology allows 'ideological formations such as Law and Religion an equal role to [that of] the economy, and even the attribution of a "supervisor" causality to them'.[53]

But on the other hand Sebastiano Timpanaro, an Italian Marxist, in an essay which was first published in 1966, challenges some of the conventional assumptions of 'vulgar materialism' found among Marxists. The concept of a socio-economic base and a purely epiphenomenal superstructure of ideas and culture is, he points out, one which needs handling with care. In rejecting the idealist claim 'that the only reality is that of the Spirit and that cultural facts are in no way dependent on economic structure' it is a mistake to go to the other extreme and assume that the socio-economic infrastructure *directly* and immediately produces every idea or cultural event, in a simply mechanistic way. He points out that not only did Engels declare 'that it would be naïve to think that each single superstructural fact was the repercussion of a change in the infrastructure', but that 'Marx himself, in the 1859 preface to *A Critique of Political Economy*, explicitly affirms the dependence of the superstructure on the structure *only* "in its macroscopic and catastrophic aspects, so to speak, that is, in relation to social revolutions".'[54]

The procedure followed by Weber in his comparative studies in the sociology of religion was to identify what seemed to him a highly significant factor in the emergence of the spirit of capitalism in northern Europe, namely the Protestant ethic or 'rational worldly asceticism'. He then accounted for the non-emergence of any similar spirit of capitalist entrepreneurship in Indian culture in terms of the 'irrationality' associated with what he took to be the important place within that culture held by Hindu religious *gurus*. There is very clearly a judgemental quality in his conclusion: 'Instead of a drive towards the rational accumulation of property and the evaluation of capitalism, Hinduism created irrational accumulation chances for magicians and soul shepherds. . . .' In short, Hindu religion lacked the kind of ethic which would lead to 'rational worldly asceticism', and therefore had failed to effect that transition to industrial capitalism in which, according to Weber, the Protestant ethic had in Europe played a significant part. Thus, in relation to India's 'failed' social revolution, Weber's position is that ideas can have a crucial role. On this important issue it is clear that not only by Lukács's criteria but also by the more precisely Marxian standards of Timpanaro, Weber's position is fundamentally different from that of Marx.

NOTES

1. Joseph A. Schumpeter, *Capitalism, Socialism and Democracy* (1962), p. 11.

2. Irving M. Zeitlin, *Ideology and the Development of Sociological Theory* (1968), p. 111f.

3. Marianne Weber, *Max Weber: A Biography* (1975), p. 25.

4. Ibid.

5. Ibid., p. 31.

6. Ibid., p. 99f.

7. Ibid., p. 134.

8. Ibid., p. 135.

9. Ibid.

10. Max Weber, *The Protestant Ethic and the Spirit of Capitalism* (1930), p. 26.

11. Bryan Turner, *Weber and Islam*, pp. 181ff.

12. Ibid., p. 183.

13. Ibid., p. 184.

14. H. H. Gerth and C. Wright Mills, *From Max Weber*, (1948), p. 35.

15. Ibid., p. 47.

16. Max Weber, *The Protestant Ethic and the Spirit of Capitalism*, p. 183.

17. Gerth and Mills, p. 280.

18. The Gross Domestic Product *per capita* (which is an indicator of a country's wealth in relation to its population) for 1970 for India was 38 (unit = pound sterling); for the USA, 1932; for the UK, 887 and for West Germany, 1467. Source, *The Times* (25 September 1972).

19. *Gesammelte Aufsätze zur Religionssoziologie,* vol. I (Tübingen, 1920–1).

20. Max Weber, *The Religion of India* (1958), p. 344ff.

21. Ibid., p. 324.

22. Ibid., p. 325.

23. Ibid.

24. *East India (Census): General Report on the Census of India 1911,* Cd. Paper 7377 (London, 1914), p. 114.

25. Ibid.

26. Weber, *Religion of India*, p. 326.

27. Ibid., p. 325.

28. Angus Maddison, *Class Structure and Economic Growth* (1971), p. 78.

29. E. A. G. Robinson, 'Economic Progress in India' in P. Chaudhuri, *Aspects of Indian Economic Development* (1971), p. 95.

30. Weber, *Religion of India*, p. 326.

31. Ibid.

32. Ibid.

33. P. K. Bhowmick, 'Four Temples in Midnapur, West Bengal', in *Man in India*, vol. 40, no. 2 (April–June 1960), pp. 81–108.

34. See, e.g., *Census of India 1961*, vol. XVI, pt. VI, nos. 1, 2, 3 and 4.

35. See note 24 above, p. 115.

36. Ibid.

37. Weber, *Religion of India*, p. 328.

38. Milton Singer, 'Religion and Social Change in India: The Max Weber Thesis, Phase Three', in *Economic Development and Cultural Change*,' vol. XIV, no. 4 (July 1966), p. 502.

39. Surendranath Banerjea, *A Nation in Making* (1925, repr. 1963), p. 130.

40. Bhupendranath Datta, *Swami Vivekananda, Patriot-Prophet* (Calcutta, 1954), p. 1.

41. K. P. Karunakaran, *Religion and Political Awakening in India* (1965), p. 98.

42. See Betty Heimann, *Facets of Indian Thought* (1964), ch. VII, 'Indian Mathematics'.

43. N. R. Chakravarti, *The Indian Minority in Burma* (1971), p. 89.

44. Ibid., p. 91.

45. K. S. Sandhu, *Indians in Malaya* (1969), p. 292.

46. S. Upadhyay, *Growth of Industries in India* (1970), p. 109.

47. D. R. Gadgil, *The Industrial Revolution of India in Recent Times* (4th edn, 1942), p. 299; see also J. Coggin Brown and Y. K. Dey, *India's Mineral Wealth* (3rd edn, 1955), pp. 194–7.

48. Raymond Owens, 'Mahisya Entrepreneurs in Howrah, West Bengal' in *Bengal: Change and Continuity*, ed. by R. and M. J. Beech, South Asia Series Occasional Paper No. 16 (Michigan State University, 1970).

49. Christopher Hill, 'Partial Historians and Total History', *Times Literary Supplement* (24 November 1972), p. 1431.

50. Zeitlin, *Ideology*, (note 2) p. 112.

51. Marianne Weber, *Max Weber*, p. 335.

52. Ibid., p. 587.

53. G. Lukács, 'Max Weber and German Sociology' in *Economy and Society*, vol. I, no. 4 (November 1972), p. 390.

54. Sebastian Timpanaro, *On Materialism* (1975), p. 143.

7 Brāhman Triumphalism

(i) *The place of the Brāhman in Hindu society*

HINDU religion was seen by Marx simply as folk religion. Its continued existence in a society made up of primitive village communities therefore, in his view, needed no explanation. The Brāhman was one of a number of village functionaries according to a major source used by Marx, which gives a list of such officials. The passage ends as follows:

> . . . The boundaryman, who preserves the limits of the village, or gives evidence respecting them in cases of dispute. The superintendent of tanks and watercourses distributes the water for the purposes of agriculture. The Brahmin, who performs the village worship. The schoolmaster, who is seen teaching the children in a village to read and write in the sand. The calendar-Brahmin, or astrologer, etc. These officers and servants generally constitute the establishment of a village . . . Under this simple form of municipal government the inhabitants of the country have lived from time immemorial.[1]

The Brāhman is therefore regarded by Marx as a village priest, a feature of the village scene, and no more. Marx knew of Manu as an ancient Hindu lawgiver[2] but he does not appear to have connected the two. Had he done so he would have perceived that the Brāhman is more than simply a village figure; he is also, in his capacity as the composer and guardian of the Sanskritic Śāstras, the representative of what has been described (using Robert Redfield's categories) as the Great Tradition. In the Indian context the Great Tradition *par excellence* is represented in the tradition of learning and the corpus of sacred texts, including for example the Law Code of Manu (*Manava Śāstra*), recited from generation to generation in the Sanskrit language, embodying the traditions of all-India Brāhmanism. In contrast to the Great Tradition, in Redfield's model, are the many Little Traditions. These consist of the great variety of local customs and folklore, different in every district, even, to some extent, in every village. The use of this Great Tradition/Little Tradition model in connection with Indian society is open to objection, especially on the grounds that while there was a single Great Tradition in the Mexican situation in which

Redfield originally formulated the model, there is no single Great Tradition in India; there are, for example, the Islamic and Christian, as well as Sanskritic-brāhmanical Great Traditions, and others besides, each with its related Little Traditions.[3] However, the model is to some extent applicable to Indian society and it does serve to indicate the over-simplification contained in the conception of Indian society as a congeries of separate, entirely self-contained village communities existing un-changed from time immemorial. In particular it highlights the faulty evaluation of the role of the Brāhman in Indian society which that conception implies. For the Brāhman, even in the most remote rural situation, was not and is not *simply* a village official. Rather he was and is the representative and the agent of a particular supra-village and supra-regional ideology. What that ideology was must now be considered briefly.

The Brāhman[4] was the bearer, transmitter, and guardian of the sacred word, the Veda, the body of Sanskrit compositions which were regarded as *śruti*, that is, as having been 'heard' by the rishis or sages of old, heard by the ear that was open to divinely inspired truth. The Veda thus takes its place among the various corpuses of the world's religious literature, each of which claims the special status of *revealed* truth not to be set aside, or disobeyed, or questioned. The Brāhman's knowledge of the words of revelation was handed on from father to son and was closely preserved and guarded so that it should not fall into the hands of non-Brāhmans. Exclusive possession of it gave the Brāhman the exclusive right to carry out all the necessary sacred rituals which, he asserted, were essential for the continuance of human life and society. The various privileges which accrued to the Brāhman in respect of this exclusive right were easily explainable, should anyone rebel against the social injustice such privileges seemed to entail. They were explained in terms of *karma*, the doctrine that a man's position and fortune in his present existence are the consequence of his deeds in past existences. Whether or not this doctrine originated among the Brāhmans (and it may not have done) it was evidently recognised by them as being of great value in the defence of the system of ritualised social stratification known generally as caste. The Indian word for such social division is *jati*, meaning literally 'birth', or in this context 'status according to birth'. Only those whose deeds in previous existences had been outstandingly correct in terms of caste duty would be born in the present existence into a Brāhman family. The Brāhman scriptures set out a schematisation of the various types of human *jati*; these 'types' were called *varnas*, each of which had its appropriate duties. The most elevated *varna* was that of the Brāhman; next was the *Kśatriya* or warrior, next came the *vaisya*, or merchant and trading class, and lowest of all the *sudra*, the labourer, upon whose labours, of course, the whole edifice rested.

Brāhmans, as the learned, the wise, the guardians of the sacred knowledge, had their special functions to perform, and even though these were not very onerous they were, so it was claimed, essential to society's well being. It was necessary to guard against having a superfluity of Brāhmans, for although they constituted a sacred order these gentlemen were not celibate but often the fathers of considerable families. It was necessary, therefore, to ensure that there was a growing demand for Brāhman skills. The best way in the long run was to extend the area of Brāhman culture.

(ii) *Brahmans as missionaries*

One of the commonest Western misconceptions concerning Hindu religion is that it is not the missionary kind. This is true only in the sense that, until very recent times, there were no Hindu missionary societies collecting coins from the faithful to finance the sending of religious agents to lands beyond the seas where they would set about changing the ways and the ideas of the inhabitants of those foreign lands. If that is what is meant by a 'missionary' religion it is true that Hindu religion cannot qualify for the title, for its missionaries are not paid from the proceeds of missionary boxes nor are their efforts entirely concentrated on lands overseas. But Hindu religion certainly has its missionaries after its own special style, and they have been at work steadily and surely within south Asia for many centuries, and to a less extent in south-east Asia.[5] As Srinivas pointed out, Hinduism proselytised without the aid of a church, through the agency of the Brāhmans.[6]

At one level the Hindu mission consists in appropriating and absorbing into the Hindu *jati* (caste) system any alien or independent group, and subjecting them thenceforth to rigid social domination. At another level it consists in the gradual penetration of non-brāhmanical culture by the standards and values of the Brāhmans, that is, the Sanskritic Great Tradition. In this way the Brāhmanical type of society was continually extended. The process still continues today to some extent, probably by sheer cultural momentum.

The process has been variously described as Hinduisation, Sanskriti-sation and Brāhmanisation. Srinivas, in his study of the Coorgs of south

India, introduced the term Sanskritisation.[7] As used by Srinivas the term implies something like entry into a league table in which social groups, that may be differentiated by tribes or occupations or in some other way, enter into competition with others for social position, the Brāhmans always remaining the supreme caste. If one group somewhere near the bottom of the scale manages to move up a little and successfully presses a claim to be socially superior to some other group, then, as Srinivas says, 'another comes down, but all this takes place in an essentially stable hierarchical order. The system itself does not change.'[8] The Brāhmans remain supreme for they are the sacred order, the bearers of the knowledge by means of which all these things are ordered.

According to the Law of Manu, the members of a higher caste were not to demean themselves by doing the work of a lower caste, and a low caste was not allowed to encroach on the occupational rights of a higher, although in cases of necessity higher castes could undertake lower caste work. 'One main object was undoubtedly to maintain the Brāhmans in a privileged position as a sacrosanct order with a monopoly of learning', observed O'Malley. 'This opinion they long maintained, and under early Hindu rule they were like the clergy of the Catholic Church in medieval times, who, as Froude points out in *Times of Erasmus and Luther*, reigned supreme over prince and peasant by the magic of sanctity, had the monopoly of learning, and enjoyed the secular power which learning, combined with sanctity and assisted by superstition, can bestow.'[9]

By persuading others that they were the bearers and guardians of the Sanskritic 'eternal truth' (*sanatana dharma*) and securing their hold on secular power, the Brāhmans were the catalysts in a process of the diffusion of caste ideas and values. For example, manual labour was despised by higher castes and performed by lower castes only. This has become a cultural value in India (although not unknown elsewhere) which has proved very hard to eradicate. Manual labour is degrading; manual workers are inferior people and should in all things defer to scholars and gentlemen; such was the scale of values which a religious ideology succeeded in maintaining for many centuries; it retains its hold in places where Sanskrit learning survives.

(iii) *Monarchy, monopoly and orthodoxy in pre-Muslim India*

Brāhmanical religion is seen at its most characteristic in the period *before* it came into widespread contact with Islam in the Indian sub-continent from about 1000 CE; it was modified as a result of that encounter, as well as by its later encounter with Catholic missions from the sixteenth century onwards, and, later still, with Protestant chaplaincies and missions in the period of the British Raj from the early nineteenth century onwards. It probably reached full autonomous development in the Gupta period in the fourth century AD, a period sometimes described as the golden age of Hindu culture and civilisation. What is now known of the great glory of the Gupta empire (largely as a result of the research carried out by modern historians of India) enables us to recognise the continuation of the large-scale politically organised Hindu civilisation which can be seen at least as early as the third century BC in the Maurya empire of northern and central India. Considerable power was in the hands of the Brāhmans as the learned and priestly élite who enjoyed much respect and prestige. It is in this, the classical period, that the 'pure type' of the Brāhman is to be found.

A manual of statecraft from the Mauryan empire has survived. Entitled simply *Artha Śāstra*, or Treatise on Government, it was composed by a Brāhman priest, a minister of state, named Kautilya.[10] It sets out systematically the day-to-day details of a king's life, the administration of the state, and the conduct of relations with other neighbouring states. It will be useful to make a brief survey of some of the major matters with which it deals, for this will give some impression of the nature of the ideal Hindu state. The personal duties of the king are set out; he is told what ministers of state he should appoint and how they should be appointed; rules for the conducting of council meetings are given. The economic organisation of the kingdom is laid down and such matters as the maintenance of villages, division of lands, building of forts, and collection of revenue are dealt with. Various departments of state are listed, each with its minister or superintendent, departments such as commerce, agriculture, weaving, metal work, forestry, brewing, and so on. Another section deals with legal affairs such as the making of forms of agreement, and with laws regarding marriage, debts, purchases and sales, and similar matters. The procedure for trials and the drawing up of appropriate punishments is described. Foreign policy is dealt with at length: the duty and desirability of constant geographical expansion by what today is called 'territorial acquisition by military means'; consideration of who are the state's 'natural enemies' and the policies to be adopted towards them in peace and war; when to wage war and when not to, and how to deal with conquered enemies. From this the manual goes on to the obviously important subject of the army; its recruitment, equipment, encampment or billeting, and its security. Theories of battle are given considerable attention, as also are such matters as the disposition of troops in the battlefields, the work of the infantry or the cavalry, of chariots and of elephants. Finally matters such as the stirring up of dissension among enemies are dealt with; systems of espionage; how spies are to be recruited and trained for their work; counter-espionage, and so on. In the Law Code of Manu, or *Manava-Śāstra*,[11] the Brāhman is regarded 'as by right the chief of this whole creation. As such he may take a Sudra's [lowest caste] property for the purpose of sacrifice without fear of the slightest punishment.' Besides the security guaranteed him by the fact that a king may never put a Brāhman to death, whatever crimes he may commit, the Brāhman enjoys various other legal prerogatives.[12]

Such was the Brāhmanical state, for there is no reason to suppose that these manuals were made and preserved through the centuries and never used. He would be naïve indeed who accepted the suggestion of some modern exponents of Brāhmanism that the Brāhmanical state never actually existed, and that the statecraft which Brāhman writers evidently spent so much time elaborating was never actually employed. To maintain that Kautilya, the author of the *Artha Śāstra*, renowned not only as a king-maker and inaugurator of the Mauryan dynasty but also 'for being the greatest Indian exponent of the art of government, the duties of kings, ministers and officials, and the methods of diplomacy',[13] never actually had any practical experience of these things would be to strain credibility too far. Moreover the system of government described in the *Artha Śāstra* is confirmed by much of what is known about the India of the third century BC from the writings of the Greek diplomat, Megasthenes, who resided in India at the court of Chandragupta as the representative of Seleucus I, and by the evidence provided by the epics and other early documents and inscriptions.[14] Under powerful emperors such as the Mauryas and the Guptas it was just this kind of civilisation which was built up, and it was the Brāhmans who were its architects and preservers. They successfully legitimated their position of power by their highly sophisticated philosophical theory, having persuaded other classes, and the king in particular, that they were the ritual specialists who were indispensible to the whole scheme.

The transmission of this Brāhman ideology of the state from India to other parts of Asia, especially to the east of India, appears to have begun in approximately the first century CE. There is plenty of evidence of the eastward progress of cultural influence. The ruins of massive temples such as Angkor Wat in Cambodia or Borobudur in Java; the many remains of statues of Hindu gods, such as Vishnu and Shiva; the influence of Sanskrit in the place names, the family names and the languages of these countries; and above all the elaborate construction of royal capitals and palaces to represent in architectural form the Hindu cosmology, in which the king in his house is the centre of the universe, are some of the principal forms this evidence takes.

It was the Brāhmans who played a large part in bringing about the disappearance of Buddhism from India. Their hostility towards Buddhists is attested in the manuals of government which have already been mentioned. While it is laid down by the Brāhman author of the *Laws of Manu*, for example, that the king has a duty to worship Brāhmans (defined as those who know the Veda – the orthodox Brāhmanical scriptures), it is also laid down that he has a duty to banish instantly from his realm any men belonging to a heretical sect (that is, who do not regard the Veda as the source of all truth as the Buddhists did not): 'Let the king, after rising early in the morning, worship *brāhmans* who are well versed in the threefold sacred science and learned in polity, and follow their advice. Let him daily worship aged brāhmans who know the Veda. . . .'[15] But, 'gamblers, dancers, and singers, cruel men, *men belonging to an heretical sect*, those following forbidden occupations and sellers of spiritous liquor, let him instantly banish from his town'.[16]

As Lalmoni Joshi has recently pointed out:

> . . . the fact of Brāhmanical hostility to Buddhism has not usually been given the attention it deserves. Right from the days of the Buddha the orthodox 'Hindus' (the followers of Vedic, Brāhmanical and Pauranic religious doctrines and practices) have been showing a bitter hostility towards Buddha's teachings. This hostile attitude was vigorously sustained till Buddhism was overpowered in India and disappeared from the land of its birth.[17]

It was the Buddhist *Sangha*, or religious order, that was the special target for the Brāhmans' attack. The Buddhist lay-people could more easily be dealt with and brought back within the all-encompassing bounds of Hinduised caste society once the Sangha had been destroyed, for it was to the Sangha that the people looked for guidance and teaching, and because the Sangha represented virtually all their aspirations as Buddhists.

Popularity attracts jealousy. This is what appears to have happened in the case of Indian Buddhism. Although it is always possible to find exceptions, in general the attitude of the Brāhmans was one of unwillingness to share royal patronage and political and cultural influence with non-brāhmanical sects. The stronger the kingdom the more important it became for Brāhmans to establish and maintain their own position at court and in the kingdom at large.

The triumph of the Brāhmans in twelfth-century India[18] was short-lived, however. The Muslims, when they had succeeded in invading the northern plains and establishing camps which eventually became towns, were able to consolidate their positions with remarkable speed; one of the major factors was their superior skill at arms and the speed at which they could move on horseback compared with the lumbering operations of Hindu rajahs on elephants. Moreover the brāhmanical Hindu states of northern India were apparently incapable of co-operating and presenting a united front to the invaders from the north-west.

Thus north India, and then eventually much of central India and the peninsula, came under Muslim control. Here and there Hindu states survived, notably in the kingdom of Vijayanagar in south India. But the period from about the end of the twelfth to the middle of the eighteenth century was in India one of Muslim dominance; Hindu civilisation as it had once existed was in eclipse, and certainly Brāhman cultural and religious dominance was literally put out of court. During the whole period of Muslim rule the control which Brāhmans had exercised over unorthodox religious teachers *(gurus)* and their followers came practically to an end, with the result that many such devotional or salvation cults began to flourish and the status and power of the gurus grew 'to grotesque heights'.[19] But many of the inhabitants of Bengal were very willing to become Muslims and in doing so found a dignity which was denied them by their self-styled Hindu 'superiors'.

It might be thought that the Muslims, once they had gained political ascendancy in India, would have suppressed this growth of what to pious orthodox Muslims would undoubtedly have appeared as pagan and idolatrous practices. Sometimes this was the case, but quite often it was not. The real tension was between the Muslim rulers and the Brāhmans. As an historian of Bengal has shown, in a socio-political study of the reign of Husain Shah in Bengal,[20] even as late as the sixteenth century the Brāhmans, now completely bereft of political influence for some centuries, had still not reconciled themselves to Muslim rule and displayed a sullen bitterness towards the Mughals. The Hindus of Bengal were led to believe that Brāhmans would one day gain political power and end Muslim rule (as actually happened for a short time during the reign of Raja Ganesha in the fifteenth century). Thus the threat to Islamic power during this period in India came not directly from folk cults but from the embittered Brāhmans by whom the Muslim rulers knew themselves to be seriously challenged. They could, therefore, hardly have been expected to feel very friendly towards the Brāhmans, and it is this situation of conflict which largely explains the strained relations between the two groups, even though the Muslim ruling class found it necessary to make use of Brāhmans in the administration of their territory, and the Brāhmans found it necessary to accept such employment in order to make a living. It is significant that wherever they could the Muslim rulers appear to have made appointments to local administrative posts from the Kayastha caste rather than from the Brāhmans. The Kayastha were a landowning caste with a high rate of literacy; in Bengal they made notable contributions to the vernacular literature of this period. As Tarafdar points out, whether or not the Muslim rulers made it their deliberate policy to support the Kayasthas with the object of diminishing Brāhmanical influence is not clear, but in any case the increasing part played by the Kayastha intelligentsia and landlords must have had that effect.[21]

(iv) *Brāhmanism at the beginning of British rule*

The Brāhmanical states of ancient India were centres from which Brāhmanical culture grew outwards. Neither at the beginning of Muslim rule nor at its end in the eighteenth century had they succeeded in extending over the whole land of India. At the beginning of British rule there were still places where no trace of Brāhman culture was to be found. A vivid description of one such area was given by John Woodroffe writing as late as 1918:

> I write this on a high plateau in Palamau, and look across a wide stretch of tall grass with tips of waving silver, the home, until about nine years ago (when the place was first opened) of the wild bison. The green and silver of the prairie is splashed here and there with patches of orange flower, which the blazing sun jewels with its points of light. The near distance shows the water of a mountain tarn and two clumps of trees – the grove of worship of the ancient Kolarian peoples. Here a sparse remnant adore today, as did their ancestors thousands of years ago. Of Brāhmanism or other Aryan faith, there is no sign.[22]

Thus the religious situation in India at the beginning of British rule was that the Brāhmanical–Sanskritic tradition had established itself over large areas of the sub-continent, but not uniformly. There were large upland and forest areas where, as in the part of Chotanagpur described by Woodroffe, no trace of Brāhmanism was found, and even in those places where it was known it was not always the dominant religious element by any means. In some parts of India, in eastern Bengal for example, and the Punjab, Muslims were the dominant religious community. The British who came to India in increasing numbers from the latter part of the eighteenth century understood this aspect of the religious situation well enough: the Muhammedans, as they called them, constituted the great and notable exception to the otherwise universally prevailing 'religion of the Hindoos'.

Consider, for example, the following passage from a work published in London in 1834:[23]

> In considering any tribe or family of mankind, our view would be eminently imperfect were religion omitted; but in the case of the Hindoo, the omission is impracticable, since it is his religion, and nothing else, that renders him what he is. By penetrating, therefore, if it be possible, to the core of his religious institutions, by studying the relations which in India appear to have always subsisted between sacred things and civil, we can alone hope to comprehend the Hindoo character.[24]

The writer goes on to say that, quite apart from the necessity of understanding the religion of the people of India in order to understand India, the subject has an importance of its own in a world context, for:

> it can never be regarded as a matter of trifling curiosity to endeavour to comprehend those modes of faith which influence the condition of four hundred millions of human beings – more than one-third of the whole human race being still Hindoos in religion.[25]

The account of Hindu religion which then follows is based on the writings of British and French Indologists such as Sir William Jones, Colebrook and the Abbé Dubois, who in turn based their accounts of Hinduism largely on literary sources, notably the Sanskrit Vedic texts of the Brāhmans.

Even this account of 1834, biased as it is in favour of the notion that for the 'people of India' there is the appropriate 'religion of India', is compelled to take account of empirical evidence to the contrary; evidence provided by the account of his travels given by Buchanan, for example. Thus in certain regions, the writer notes, some tribes exist who have 'never adopted the Brāhmanical creed'. But clearly these are regarded as exceptional rather than normal.

The idea that there is 'a religion' to which the inhabitants of India adhere is common to late eighteenth- and early nineteenth-century British writers; Holwell,[26] for example, refers to 'the principles and worship of the Hindoos'; Dow speaks of 'the learning, religion and philosophy of the Brāhmans' which he equates with 'the mysterious religion of Hindostan', and 'the learning of the Hindoos';[27] William Jones regards 'the religion of Brāhma' as having 'prevailed' for a very long time throughout the great extent of Upper India;[28] and so on. In general the tendency is to regard the *Brāhmanical*, textually based tradition as the prevailing religion, and to see it as imposed on the people from above by the Brāhmans, whose earlier association with political power was known to British Indologists.

It is this crucial point which Marx, in his account of the religion of India in the 1850s, failed to deal with. The impression given by his writing on India is that he was so preoccupied with the principle of the self-sufficient, self-contained 'village republics', the basis of what he believed to be the Asiatic mode of production, that he too easily accepted the *appropriate* form of religion in such village communities as being of the kind which a purely local village functionary could have provided. Such a village religion would have had no dimensions that reached out beyond the village. In this way Marx appears to have missed an important clue to the way in which religion functioned in India. Had he followed it up he would have discovered the nexus which existed between the Brāhmanical religion of the village and the Brāhmanical religion of the state; he would have been alerted to the continuing political role and to the very considerable economic interests of Brāhman orthodoxy in India. He would have found, not a rustic religion rooted simply in the conditions of primitive peasant life, but a state ideology which it was in the interests of Brāhmans to extend and to impose wherever possible, a state ideology which in the nineteenth century lacked a Hindu state through which to function, and which was therefore only waiting for the opportunity which would bring one into existence.

NOTES

1. K. Marx, 'The British Rule in India', *NYDT* (25 June 1853).

2. Marx knew of Manu as an ancient lawgiver, as his remark about Sir Charles Wood as 'the modern Manu' reveals; see *On Colonialism*, pp. 28, and 315.

3. See Imtiaz Ahmad, 'For a Sociology of India' in *Muslim Communities*

of South Asia, ed. by T. N. Madan (1977), p. 176.

4. For fuller accounts of what follows concerning Brāhmanism see, for example, Surendranath Dasgupta, *A History of Indian Philosophy*, vol. I (1957), ch. II, and D. D. Kosambi, *The Culture and Civilisation of Ancient India* (1965), especially ch. 7.

5. See T. O. Ling, 'Hinduism (Introduction into South-East Asia)' in *A Dictionary of Comparative Religion*, ed. by S. G. F. Brandon (1970), p. 331f.

6. See M. N. Srinivas, *Religion and Society among the Coorgs of South India* (1952), p. 212ff.

7. See note 6.

8. *Social Change in Modern India* (1966), p. 7.

9. L. S. S. O'Malley, *India's Social Heritage* (1934, repr. 1975), p. 21.

10. R. Shamasastry, *Kautilya's Arthasastra* (8th edn, 1967).

11. See *The Laws of Manu*, trans. by G. Bühler, Sacred Books of the East, vol. XXV (1886).

12. D. E. Smith, *India as a Secular State* (1963), p. 297f.

13. Shamasastry, p. v.

14. Ibid., p. vi.

15. *Laws of Manu*, VII, 37, 38.

16 *Laws of Manu*, IX, 225.

17. Lalmoni Joshi, *Studies in the Buddhistic Culture of India* (1967), p. 394.

18. The same process occurred in both Kerala and Bengal at about the same period. See Trevor Ling, 'Buddhism in Bengal' in *Man and His Salvation*, ed. by E. Sharpe and J. R. Hinnells (1973), and Cyriack Pullapilly, 'The Izhavas of Kerala and their Historic Struggle for Acceptance in the Hindu Society', *Religion and Social Conflict in South Asia*, ed. by Bardwell L. Smith (1976).

19. Max Weber, *The Religion of India* (1958), p. 325; see also p. 88 above.

20. Momtazur Rahman Tarafdar, *Husain Shahi Bengal 1494–1538: A Sociopolitical Study* (1965).

21. Tarafdar, p. 193.

22. John Woodroffe, *Śakti and Śākta* (1918), p. xi.

23. *The Library of Entertaining Knowledge: the Hindoos*, vol. I, (Anon, 1834).

24. Ibid., p. 142

25. Ibid., 400 million would have been a gross over-estimate for the 1830s.

26. See P. J. Marshall, *The British Discovery of Hinduism in the Eighteenth Century* (1970), ch. 1, p. 48.

27. Ibid., p. 107.

28. Ibid., p. 252.

Part Three

Beyond Marx

8 The Persistence of Religion

MARX, like Auguste Comte and a number of other intellectuals in the nineteenth century, believed that wherever modern science and technology penetrated, religion was doomed. It might persist for a while, but it could have no real vitality left in the modern world; its last spasmodic strugglings would soon be ended and it would lie still.

Such has not been the case. Religion survives the spread of science, and scientists are among those who continue to adhere to religion. In terms of the Marxist analysis this can be explained by the fact that capitalism lasted longer than Marx had supposed it would; the communist revolution, for which, in 1847, he believed industrial Europe was ripe, failed to arrive. Capitalism persisted and therefore, as its heavenly reflex, religion persisted.

One would not expect religion to survive among Marxists however. One would not expect it to survive in a communist society. One would not expect it to survive among militant revolutionaries keen to overthrow capitalism and imperialism. Yet all these things have happened. The 'religiosity' of Marxists, which has been widely commented upon is, it is true, a controversial issue. Those who hold themselves to be enlightened, rational and scientifically minded beings understandably resent the allegation that their devotion to the cause has anything in common with 'religion' in the generally accepted sense of the word, or at least in the sense generally accepted among many Marxists. The use of 'religion' as a pejorative term for those beliefs, attitudes and activities which are viewed with disfavour and even contempt is however not confined to Marxists. It is a recurrent theme in the history of religion, at least from the time of the Hebrew prophets and up to the time of the great neo-orthodox theologian of the twentieth century, Karl Barth. It was characteristic also of his theologically liberal compatriot, Rudolf Bultmann. 'Religionless Christianity' was, in the 1960s, seen by religious radicals as the only true Christianity. But what persisted, purged of rituals and sacraments, was a form of belief which Marx had considered to be doomed to an early death if it was not artificially sustained by the state.

Moreover, to an extent which would perhaps have seemed highly unlikely to nineteenth-century intellectuals, religion has persisted in conventional forms. Not only has this occurred among those sections of society who have always adhered to traditional habits of belief and practice, but also among modern, urban, educated classes in industrial societies. Nor has this happened only in the capitalist world. It has happened in the Soviet Union and, at the time of writing towards the end of the 1970s, there is no sign of the religion's imminent decease there but rather the reverse, as the reader will see from some of the evidence to be produced in the next chapter.

Another example of the persistence of religious beliefs, attitudes and practices where this might not have been expected can be found in India. Such persistence is illustrated in the life of a young Indian who was justly acclaimed one of the most accomplished and intellectually eminent students his tutors at Cambridge had known, namely Aurobindo Ghose. Early in his career, out of opposition to British imperialism, he took to revolutionary activities. When he was born Karl Marx was still alive; Aurobindo entered St Paul's school in London the year after Marx died.

(ii) *A product of Victorian England*

Aurobindo Ghose was born in 1872. His father, Krishna Dhan Ghose, was a graduate of the Medical College of Calcutta and had pursued higher medical studies, between 1869 and 1871, in England where he had become enamoured of all things English, and an atheist. When Aurobindo was born in Calcutta the year after his return, Ghose senior decided that the boy should be taught English language and manners, and to that end employed as nurse for the child an Englishwoman named Miss Paget. At the age of five Aurobindo was sent off to school at Loretto Convent in Darjeeling, a place intended mainly for the education of the children of British officials in India. After two years in the Convent school his father arranged something which in his eyes was even more desirable; Aurobindo and his two brothers were brought to England to continue their education. For the next fourteen years, that is, until he was twenty-one, Aurobindo lived in Shakespeare Street, Manchester; in St Stephen's Avenue, Shepherd's Bush; in Cromwell Road, South Kensington; Kempsford Gardens, Earls Court; King's College, Cambridge; and Burlington Road, Bayswater.

In Manchester he and his brothers lived with a certain William Drewett, described by his biographer[1] as 'a congregational priest'; that is, he was minister of Stockport Road Congregational Church. It was considered that Aurobindo was too young to attend school, so he was taught at home by Mrs Drewett. She taught him 'history, geography, arithmetic and French'. She taught him to read the Bible, of course, and also Shakespeare, Shelley and Keats. He seems not to have played any games; he remembers having played cricket but, as his biographer puts it, 'without much success'. Mrs Drewett wished also to make a Christian of him and save his soul, but he appears to have resisted this. Later he was taken to a convention meeting at Keswick where he was approached by an evangelist and asked if he were saved. He says in his account of the incident that he was in fact feeling rather bored and said nothing; this was received as silent admission of his conversion and much offering of thanks to God followed. He adds that he was infinitely relieved to get back to Manchester.

In September 1884 Aurobindo and his brothers were moved to London and Aurobindo was admitted to St Paul's School, just at the time when Engels, also living in London, was starting on the task of sorting out and arranging the vast amount of literary material left by Marx on his death the previous year.[2] At first Aurobindo and his brothers lodged with William Drewett's mother in Shepherd's Bush, but one day, when she was reading aloud from the Bible, Aurobindo made some disparaging remarks about Moses which so enraged the old lady that they had to leave, as she refused to live under the same roof with heretics. They moved to a large, five-storeyed house in Cromwell Road which was at that time the South Kensington office of the Liberal Club. Conditions of life were far from comfortable. The rooms in that house were large and draughty[3] and there was the constant clatter from electric trains behind the house (which Aurobindo mentions); for him there was virtually nothing in the way of a proper bed, while his diet consisted each day of bacon, tea and bread in the morning, and a sandwich and a cup of tea in the afternoon. Added to this he possessed no overcoat to offset the rigours of an unheated room and the London winter. These things are mentioned in order to establish that there was little in Aurobindo's experience of English life to make *him* enamoured of it, whatever its effect may have been on his father. Nor did things improve very much when he and his brothers moved to Earls Court, where their room overlooked a cemetery and they were able to watch funeral processions day after day.[4]

(iii) *Aurobindo at Cambridge*

His school work at St Paul's consisted mainly of classics, but in addition to this he did a great deal of reading in English and French literature and in the history of Europe. He learnt 'Italian, some German and a little Spanish'.[5] He won an open scholarship to Cambridge, and while he was there proved himself more than the equal of the majority of his English contemporaries. He was placed high in the first class in part one of the classical Tripos; his tutor's comment was that he 'possessed a knowledge of English literature far beyond the average of undergraduates and wrote a much better English than most young Englishmen'.[6] He is said also to have written Greek and Latin verse occasionally. Culturally it is clear which world he was most at home in at the age of twenty. His father's intentions for him had been more than adequately fulfilled. In the view of his biographer and disciple it was these years in England which were 'the most formative in his cultural make-up and intellectual equipment'.[7] He formed, it is said, an attachment to European and English thought; but *not* to England. It is quite clear also that he felt no attraction whatever towards religion, that is, the religion of England, which he appears to have regarded as highly objectionable and entirely ridiculous. Aurobindo's intellectual position when he left Cambridge was in several ways similar to Marx's when the latter left the University of Berlin fifty years earlier. Both were imbued with nineteenth-century European rationalist and evolutionist ideas (Darwin's formulation of such ideas was not the first that the nineteenth century had heard of them); both were critical of the social and political conditions around them; and both regarded with the same hostility a religion which consisted in the state's protection of a wooden Biblical literalism. Aurobindo had been disqualified from entry into the Indian Civil Service (according to his own explanation) on account of certain 'revolutionary' speeches he had made at the Cambridge Majlis Society, although as Leonard Gordon observes, 'a consideration of such speeches is nowhere to be found in the government files'.[8]

That is not to say that Aurobindo did not make revolutionary speeches while he was at Cambridge. His biographer tells us that he 'advocated the cause of Indian freedom in the "Majlis" in very strong language.'[9] In his preparation for the ICS examination he had studied the history of India as well as Bengali (which he had to learn as a foreign language) and Sanskrit. He had also begun to read some of the volumes of the *Sacred Books of the East*. India was beginning to take hold not only of his imagination but also of his emotions. Britain on the other hand, the land of his enforced adoption, was for him largely associated with loneliness, privation, religious fanaticism, poverty and ill-health.[10] Now he was learning that the Victorian British were not only, as it seemed to him, careless and even contemptuous of the few Indians in their midst, they were also the oppressors of the multitudes of Indians in India. The seeds of the bitter hostility to British imperial rule and of the passionate attachment to Mother India had been sown, and they were soon to grow and blossom.

(iv) *Aurobindo's political journalism*

He returned to India at the beginning of 1893 to enter the service of the Gaekwar of Baroda. Here his ability as a writer soon began to show itself. From August 1893 to February 1894 he contributed a series of articles for a Bombay weekly, *Induprakash*, in which he criticised the moderate middle-class policies of the Indian National Congress and called for more positive revolutionary action. The articles caused a considerable stir and the editor was warned by the British government that he might be prosecuted for issuing seditious literature. Aurobindo was asked to write in milder tones in future. He thereupon lost interest in the series. He did, however, eventually produce a second series of articles, published in July and August of 1894, on the Bengali nationalist, Bankim Chandra Chatterjee, who had died on 8 April of that year.

Bankim Chandra had been regarded as the leading figure in the second phase of the Bengal renaissance. The first phase was one characterised by a rediscovery of what was represented as India's *religious* and cultural heritage, the Vedic Samhitas and Upanishads. In that first stage it was, as we saw earlier, the new evaluation of the religious anti-materialist mythology and philosophy of India which provided the means for the recovery of national and, particularly, Hindu pride after centuries of Mughal rule followed by British military conquest. This had met the need felt by educated Indians, and particularly Bengalis, during the greater part of the nineteenth century, which has been called 'the need for the conviction of cultural equivalence'. The second phase was markedly more political than philosophical. Bankim Chandra has been characterised as a humanist, a socialist, and a nationalist.[11] He was the author of the song, *Bande Mataram* (Hail to thee, Mother), which became the battle hymn of the nationalists and was banned by the British authorities in India for some years. For the twenty-two-year-old Aurobindo he was the great hero of India's revolutionary reawakening. It was Bankim's criticism of the meekness and mildness of the Indian National Congress politicians which Aurobindo was now echoing, and it was Bankim's political doctrine which provided the inspiration for the extremist position which Aurobindo was beginning to adopt. Bankim, it has been said, was 'the brightest luminary in the firmament of renascent Bengal . . . the high priest of nationalism in India'.[12] Aurobindo, when he was at the height of his own political activity, acknowledged the lasting influence of Bankim Chandra: 'Of the new spirit that is leading the nation to resurgence and independence Bankim is the inspirer and political guru.'[13]

It was from about 1902 that Aurobindo's interest in political *action*, as distinct from pamphleteering, began to show clearly. For eight years since his arrival in Baroda he had been engaged in his own 'discovery of India'. As he explored the culture of the native land from which he had for twenty years been alienated, and as he contemplated the servile condition of his fellow Indians under British rule, two features of Indian culture began to attract him. One was yoga, the practice of which he took up during these years at Baroda in order to increase his own mental and physical powers. 'I learnt', he wrote, 'that Yoga gives power, and I thought why the devil should I not get the power and use it to liberate my country.'[14] The other item of Indian tradition which increasingly fascinated him was the *Shakta* tradition – that is, the tradition of devotion to the great divine Mother as the source of infinite energy and power. (The word *shakta* is the common Indian word for 'power' or 'ability'.) By 1905 he had forged this traditional idea of *Shakta* into an instrument of immediate political and revolutionary action.

For in that year he produced a document entitled *Bhawani mandir*. This was 'for private circulation only' setting out a plan for the 'rebirth' of India. By rebirth he meant, as he said expressly in the document, 'the re-aryanisation' of India. 'Bhawani' is the divine mother, *Shakti*, strength, and her children must erect for her a new, true sanctuary (*mandir*) in India. The failure of India was due to failure to possess Shakti; 'The one essential thing" he wrote, was 'strength'. It was not knowledge that was needed, not love, or enthusiasm, but strength.[15] Some of the paragraph headings in the document will provide an indication of its mood and general tenor:

> We in India fail in all things for want of Shakti; our knowledge is a dead thing for want of Shakti; our bhakti (devotion) cannot live and work for want of Shakti: India therefore needs Shakti alone; India, grown old and decrepit, has to be reborn; what is a nation? – the Shakti of its millions; it is our own choice whether we create a nation or perish; India must be reborn, because her birth is demanded by the future world.[16]

The appeal of the argument is intensely nationalistic. The means by which nationalistic ends were to be achieved was the Shakti cult – the worship of the divine mother, India. Over against *her* cult there was the barbarism of the Mleccha, the foreigner. There are certain important complications in this emphasis on Shakti which need to be made clear. India's decline is seen from the Shakti point of view as being due to neglect of the classical doctrines of Shaktism in favour of the more popular and emotional religion of Vaishnavism, that erotic devotion to Krishna in identity with his mistress Rādha, which in the view of the Bengali Brāhmins had emasculated Bengal during the late medieval and early modern period and left her an easy prey to Muslim and British conquerors. It was not that Hindus were inferior: it was simply that they had neglected the traditional, classical source of power, devotion to *Shakti*; so the argument goes. Moreover, as J. H. Broomfield has pointed out, the Shakti mythology was predominantly the belief system of the Hindu upper castes in Bengal:

> this was an exclusive myth which reduced popular Hindu beliefs to the level of degraded survivals of medieval cults, and which gave an obvious sanction for continued high-cast Hindu dominance. In its chauvinism it classed all non-Hindus as inferior, and inculcated the virtue of struggle against aliens and alien cultures.[17]

However Aurobindo was prepared to acknowledge the value of one foreign exemplar, especially since this was an Asian country – Japan. Just as Japan had become strong by recourse to a religious nationalism, so too, argued Aurobindo, must India. The document then outlined plans for the creation of a new order of yogins who would be dedicated to the development of Shakti and the regeneration of India. It is probably to be understood as a political revolutionary document disguised in religious terminology.

The priorities for Aurobindo during this period are, as Gordon has observed, quite clear: 'Aurobindo placed politics before religion, although he often couched his political writing and speeches in religious phraseology'.[18] During these last few years in Baroda, from 1902 to 1906, he was in touch with B. G. Tilak and a number of revolutionaries in western India. Together with other political extremists he was involved in plans to capture the Congress from the moderates who were at that time its leaders. His attention began to turn towards his native Bengal for he said 'what Bengal thinks tomorrow, India will be thinking tomorrow week'. His idea at that time, he says, 'was an armed revolution in the whole of India'. He sees in retrospect that what happened was that the Bengalis were unwilling to wait until the time was ripe; they engaged in childish activities such as 'killing a magistrate, and so on', and so the movement ran out into 'terrorism and dacoities which were not at all my idea or intention'.[19] He wanted something bigger.

(v) *Political action and imprisonment*

On 20 July 1905 the Government Act providing for the partition of Bengal into east and west was passed. This was immediately followed, especially in Bengal, by a tremendous civil and political agitation, notably the Swadeshi and Swaraj movements, and aroused many to political activism who had been indifferent or relatively inactive until then. From early in 1906 onwards, except for a brief period of return to Baroda to wind up his affairs there, Aurobindo was in Bengal. He wrote a number of political articles, and delivered many political speeches. In these he increasingly made use of concepts and terms derived from Indian religion and mythology. But nationalism was his ultimate concern. The divine energy was behind the Indian nationalist movement; India excelled in spirituality; therefore it was Indian spirituality to which attention must be given, for this was to be the agency by means of which India's supremacy would be established.[20] For him, as for many others, the newly discovered, neo-Vedantic Brāhmaniṣm was very attractive. 'We recognise no political objective except the divinity of our Motherland', he wrote, 'no present object of political endeavour except liberty, and no method or action as political good or evil except as it truly helps or hinders our progress towards our national emancipation.'[21] His articles began to be censored by the police and his political speechmaking and activities closely watched.

His career as a revolutionary in Bengal lasted altogether four years, from early 1906 to February 1910. But he was actively engaged for a total of only two years, that is, from 1906 until his arrest in May 1908. On 4 May his house in Calcutta was searched by the police and he was arrested and imprisoned in Alipore Jail. It was during this period in Alipore Jail that Aurobindo began to practise yoga based on the Bhagavad-Gita, and to meditate, as he says, 'with the help of the Upanishads'. He began also to see visions and to hear voices, such as the voice of Vivekananda.[22]

It is important to establish clearly that it was while he was in prison that Aurobindo began to undergo experiences of a religious nature, or to undergo experiences which he, from *that* time onwards, interpreted in religious terms. These are recorded in his prison diary which he wrote immediately after his release. There was an interval of nine months between his release from prison in May 1909 and the sudden imminence of re-arrest by the British police in February 1910. He had already, *well before the incidents of 1910* and his flight from British India, moved in the direction of a new, religious, personal alignment. In other words, he did not suddenly discover the value of a religious 'pose' in the face of imminent arrest and re-imprisonment. Those nine months were in fact a period of political disillusionment.

For the twelve months which had elapsed up to the time of his release from jail on 6 May 1909 had seen a remarkable decline in Indian revolutionary zeal. The government now had the situation well in hand, and the agitation for self-rule (*Swaraj*) and the boycott of British goods (*Swadeshi*) had lost much of their earlier impetus. In his prison diary, *Karakahini*, he relates that he came out of jail a new man as a result of his sufferings on the one hand, on the other of the visions he had seen and the heavenly voices he had heard.[23] It seemed, however, that the new man had come too late. He himself has recorded the strong sense of anticlimax which was now to be felt.

> I looked round when I came out, I looked round for those to whom I had been accustomed to look for counsel and inspiration. I did not find them. There was more than that. When I went to jail the country was alive with the cry of *Bande Mataram*, alive with the hope of a nation, the hope of millions of men who had newly risen out of degradation. When I came out of jail, I listened for that cry, but there was instead a silence.[24]

Meetings which had formerly been held in College Square, a large open space in central Calcutta, used to be attended by Bengalis in their thousands. 'We continued to hold our political meetings in College Square', he records. 'In all there used to be about a hundred persons, that too, mostly passers-by.'[25] This cannot have been other than discouraging. A political conference in Hooghly District in September kept him occupied for a while and then, in November, he took up residence in College Square at the house of his uncle. The afternoons he spent at the office of the periodicals *Karmayogin* and *Dharma* which he had founded, although we are told there was not much work to do. It was while he was there one evening in February 1910 with a few of his friends that a rumour was received that the police were about to search the office and arrest Aurobindo. Some were prepared to make a fight of it. But Aurobindo received a heavenly warning: 'Suddenly I heard a voice from above saying, "No! go to Chandernagore". After leaving jail I used to hear voices. In those days I used to obey them without questioning.'[26] Chandernagore was at that time a French colony, an enclave where British authority could not reach; it is on the Hooghly river, a few miles upstream from Calcutta. It was in those days the quickest way out of British India from where Aurobindo and his friends were. In ten minutes Aurobindo was on the banks of the Hooghly. His companions followed at intervals, taking zig-zag routes 'to evade the surveillance of the CID men who were posted at the *Karmayogin* office'. They called out a boatman and engaged a boat to take them immediately under cover of night to Chandernagore. On arrival at the French town Aurobindo was accommodated in a friend's house. He requested that his arrival should be kept a strict secret, a request his friend readily complied with. His companions went back to Calcutta the next day, and apart from them nobody knew where Aurobindo had gone. He stayed at Chandernagore, where he was safely beyond the reach of the British, until it became clear what should be done next. 'I was thinking about what to do next', he records. 'Then I got the *Adesh* – command – to go to Pondicherry.' This, it will be remembered, was another French colony in India. Arrangements were made for the voyage to be made in complete secrecy. The man he was staying with, Motilal, wrote to a friend in Calcutta 'telling him that Sri Aurobindo wanted him to make the necessary arrangements privately so as to keep his departure secret'.[27] Various devices were used, says his biographer, 'to put the police off the scent'. Tickets were bought in other people's names, and to Colombo instead of to Pondicherry, although it was to Pondicherry that he intended to go. All went well; Aurobindo and a companion boarded the steamer as planned and left Calcutta in the early hours of 1 April 1910. They reached Pondicherry in the afternoon of 4 April, and there Aurobindo remained.

(vi) *A change of course*

The sudden withdrawal from a life of extreme political activism needed some explanation, Aurobindo felt later. He wrote, 'I came away because I did not want anything to interfere with my Yoga, and because I got a very distinct *adesh* [command] in the matter . . . I knew from within that the work [of politics] which I had begun there was destined to be carried forward . . . by others.'[28]

From that day he turned his back on personal participation in politics, and absorbed himself in the life of a yogin. It was as a yogin that he eventually turned to philosophy, in accordance with his own notion that a yogin ought to be able to turn his hand to anything. We are not here concerned with the nature of the philosophical ideas which he eventually worked out, and which came to be designated integral non-dualism. Nor are we concerned with the question which has been raised, whether his system can justly be called either 'integral' or 'non-dualist'. Our concern here has been to trace out the way by which Aurobindo, who at an earlier stage had been a political revolutionary, contemptuous of religion, came to be a yogin, a religious professional, an exponent of the mystical life and the founder of a cult which has attracted many men and women who, for one reason and another, were searching for 'the divine life', and to whom it seemed that Aurobindo had found what they were searching for.

He left the life of politics, according to his own account, because of a divine command and because God had something more important for him to do. Until that February evening in the *Karmayogin* office, however, he seems to have been fully convinced that the great cause, for which he had so recently been released from prison, was to go on fighting in the strength of the divine Mother's *Shakti*, for the freedom of the people of India from foreign rule.[29]

It is probable that he was already predisposed to abandon politics, both as a result of his painful prison experiences, and the discouragement of finding on his release that the political atmosphere had cooled so much and so many comrades had disappeared. The Hindu cult of the Divine Mother which had given shape and direction to his political activity could now itself be given the priority which formerly had been given to political action. It is significant that the religious cult he embraced was as violent as his politics had been. For *Shaktism*, more than other forms of Indian religion, approves of violent, aggressive action. Eventually a French woman whom Aurobindo met in Pondicherry, Mira Richard, became for him the Divine Mother. She settled in Pondicherry for the rest of her life and 'he idealised her as the Mother of Gods and the concrete manifestation of vast forces at work in the universe'.[30]

The major reason for Aurobindo's not returning to British India seems to have been that he knew he was likely to have been arrested if he went. As late as 1920 he was invited by Joseph Baptista, who was a barrister of Bombay and a nationalist political worker, to return to India and take up the editorship of a paper and work for the cause of national independence. Aurobindo's reply, dated 5 January 1920, was that the offer was a tempting one but could not be accepted. 'I understand', he wrote, 'that up to last September the Government of Bengal (and probably the Government of

Madras also) were opposed to my return to British India and that practically this opposition meant that if I went back I should be interned or imprisoned under one or another of the beneficent Acts which are apparently still to subsist as helps in ushering in the new era of trust and co-operation.'[31] However he had not retired to an ivory tower where he ceased to have any interest in political affairs. He retained an interest in the freedom struggle, although from a distance, and was prepared to predict that it would one day be won. His hostility to Britain, the oppressive father, and his devotion to the beloved mother whom he could worship at Pondicherry remained as strong as ever. But whereas in the earlier period of his life the political struggle had absorbed all his energies, this now gave way to his service of the Divine Mother in mystical devotion. It might be held that Aurobindo's earlier political activity on the one hand, and his mysticism on the other, should be seen as radically contrasting, *alternative* ways of giving expression to the inner attitude which underlies all his life story, namely, hostility to imperial Britain and devotion to Mother India. This might be so if politics and mysticism are to be regarded always as *ultimate* alternatives. In Aurobindo's case there is no evidence that they were thought of in this way. The latter part of his life at Pondicherry, when he was primarily engaged in mystical thought and practice, does not seem to have been regarded by him as discontinuous from the political activity of his earlier years. In that earlier period political action had provided the way in which he could canalise his feelings of devotion to the divine Mother India. When outward circumstances brought his political activity to an end, he saw the enforced change as an opportunity for embarking on a life of devotion of another kind, at a time when his energies and affections had begun to find an outlet in mystical practice. Such appears to have been Aurobindo's view of the transition. The two stages of life do not seem to have been regarded as radically contrasting. The later mystic did not repudiate the earlier political activist. The 'integral philosophy', as it is called, which he worked out during the rest of his life at Pondicherry took the whole range of men's political, social and economic life into account. As one of his disciples put it:

> Sri Aurobindo has denounced in no uncertain terms the ideal of exclusive spirituality which aims at the static realisation of the Divine through what is known as *Karmasannyasa*, that is, renunciation of life and its manifold activities. His *Essays on the Gita* bear eloquent testimony to the fact that, like Sri Krishna, Sri Aurobindo also stands for

the establishment of the Kingdom of Truth in our life on the basis of a perfect synthesis of Jnana, Karma and Bhakti – knowledge, action, and devotion.[32]

Another possible interpretation of Aurobindo's story is that it is an illustration of that kind of turning to a non-material, non-political vision of the world which sometimes occurs in the aftermath of failed political revolution. One of the outstanding studies of this kind of phenomenon is E. P. Thompson's *The Making of the English Working Class*, where local instances of Methodist growth in the eighteenth century are shown to have been of this kind. Aurobindo's case has all the qualifications for counting as a classic example of this sort. But the persistence in modern India of Hindu religion in the form of Brāhmanical philosophy cannot simply be explained in these terms. Not all those Indians of the modern, educated class who are committed to traditional religious values can be said to be suffering from political deprivation.

Aurobindo was in many ways an exceptional man. But he was also in other respects representative of many Indians who, like himself, have been fully exposed to modern learning and scientific modes of thought, either in the universities of India, Europe, America, or Australia, and who remain firmly within the Hindu thought-world. Some, of course, do not. But many do, and the causes of adherence or non-adherence to traditional religious views of life among modern Asians, as among modern Westerners, do not appear to lie within the realm of reason and logic, any more than they are to be attributed to disappointed revolutionary expectations.

In Aurobindo's case, however, at least two other dimensions of his eventual turning from politics to Indian religious philosophy need to be considered. One is socio-structural. His return from England where he had been an alien, rejected, for whatever reason, from the highly Anglicised, horse-riding Indian Civil Service, to the India where as a member of the Brāhman caste he had an assured and honoured place in society, was an experience of upward social mobility. It is not unlikely that the new status he now enjoyed as an accepted and highly ranking member of Hindu society, a Brāhman, encouraged him to think as a Brāhman and act as a Brāhman. It is clear from the diary he kept in Alipore Jail that this was the case.[33] The other possible explanation for his return to religion is to be found in the realm of personal psychology.

(vii) *Aurobindo's mother-mysticism*

The story which has been examined here is that of a man who was, in his view, deprived in childhood, deprived of what is normally a person's birthright, namely a motherland and a culture which surrounds and supports his daily life, a social community with which he can identify and which will neutralise the experience of loneliness which may assail him as an isolated individual. Instead Aurobindo was thrust into an environment which was alien to him, both socially and emotionally, and towards which he came to canalise his feelings of hatred in his hostility to the British as the oppressors of what he had begun to see from afar as his motherland, India, from whose womb he had been torn prematurely and to whom he was now able eagerly to return. The strength of the emotion which he directed towards the rediscovered Mother-India, from whom he had been alienated, is understandable. Understandable, too, is that he should see this as the pattern for all his countrymen – strength of devotion to the Mother was what was demanded for all alike, he proclaimed. And then for a time it seemed his devotion to the Mother was to be to him a source of suffering, of fear and anxiety. The enemy whom he hated and who had come between him and the Mother was still strong enough to inflict further sufferings and to throw him into a British jail, separating him from the Mother and from his service to her. But then after a while he found that the Mother could be real to him, even in a British jail. He saw visions of her and he heard her voice. And perhaps it was possible that her service was not confined to revolutionary political action; perhaps after all the great Mother did not require that of him. So when the threat of further imprisonment and suffering loomed up in February 1910, he knew that this was not the divine Mother's will for him, she wanted him to serve her and help her to gather her children to her in another way and in another place. So to Pondicherry he went, out of the cruel father's domain, to a place where the father's vengeful hand could no longer reach him.

The Mother whom Bengali Hindus think of as visiting them at Durga Puja for a few brief days, while they keep festival and celebrate her presence – the Mother who then withdraws herself for another year, so that the mood of Bengal, even modern Bengal, is, for a brief moment, tinged with sadness – this Mother Aurobindo had found after his long absence, and into her service he now threw himself with the utmost enthusiasm.

The foregoing two paragraphs are not intended as an adequate psychological interpretation of Aurobindo's return to religion, for this is a task, however fascinating, that lies beyond the competence of the present writer to carry out, although he has discussed the possibilities of such an interpretation with colleagues whose professional expertise lies in this field, and they have confirmed that there is here an interesting case for investigation on these lines. For the purposes of our present study of Marx and religion, however, the point to be made is that the expectation of Marx and others of his generation in the nineteenth century (and of some who are still found living chronologically in the twentieth century but with the mental attitudes of the nineteenth) that religion can be accounted for without residue in terms of socio-economic development may perhaps be seen as somewhat too simplistic. The persistence of religion is a phenomenon which twentieth-century ideological Marxists tend to brush aside (or even try to sweep under the carpet), but which, if examined carefully, stands as a challenge to all oversimplified monocausal explanations.

In Marxist theory, nevertheless, religion's persistence can be satisfactorily explained wherever it occurs within modern capitalist societies – simply because such societies *are* capitalist. However its persistence in what is held to be a non-capitalist society, notably in the Soviet Union, seems to be another and altogether more difficult case to explain. It can perhaps best be considered in the context of similar countercultural movements in the West. This we shall do in the next chapter.

NOTES

1. A. B. Purani, *Life of Sri Aurobindo* (1958).

2. Heinrich Gemkow *et al., Friedrich Engels: A Biography* (1972), p. 432.

3. Some fifty-five years later the present writer had personal experience of working in that house which had by then become a government office.

4. Purani, p. 8.

5. Ibid., p. 17.

6. Ibid., p. 23.

7. Ibid., p. 51.

8. Leonard Gordon in *Bengal: Change and Continuity*, South Asia Series Occasional Papers No. 16 (Michigan State University, 1971).

9. Purani, p. 25.

10. Gordon, p. 33ff.

11. N. S. Bose, *The Indian Awakening and Bengal* (1969), ch. 10.

12. Nirmal Sinha, *Freedom Movement in Bengal 1818–1904* (1968), p. 225.

13. *Bande Mataram* (16 April 1907).

14. Purani, p. 102.

15. Ibid., p. 78f.

16. Ibid., pp. 77–81.

17. J. A. Broomfield, *Elite Conflict in a Plural Society: 20th Century Bengal* (1968), p. 16f.

18. Gordon, p. 39.

19. Purani, p. 91.

20. Gordon, p. 44f.

21. A. Ghose, *The Doctrine of Passive Resistance* (1952), pp. 66–8.

22. See Gordon, p. 44f for references, and Purani, p. 120f.

23. Aurobindo, *Karakahini* (Tales of Prison Life), trans. by Sisirkumar Ghose (1974), p. 7.

24. *Karmayogin*, 1.

25. Purani, p. 125.

26. Ibid., p. 130.

27. Ibid., p. 135.

28. Ibid., p. 156.

29. Gordon, p. 54.

30. Ibid., p. 57.

31. Purani, p. 162.

32. Haridas Chaudhuri, *The Prophet of Life Divine* (1951), p. 3.

33. His prison diary *Karakahini*, as Leonard Gordon (p. 53) points out, reveals his attitude towards lower-caste fellow prisoners: 'For all his advocacy of democracy and raising of the masses, Aurobindo showed a lack of consideration and sympathy for ordinary men and a concern that he should be accorded the special treatment due to him as a political leader and a high-caste Bengali.'

9 Marx and Counterculture

BESIDES the reasons for serious engagement with the theories of Marx and the phenomenon called Marxism given at the beginning of this book, there is another, subsidiary reason which has more to do with students themselves than with their subjects of study, and that is to be found in the nature of the widespread rejection by some recent student generations of the values and attitudes of conventional Western society. It will be useful to consider briefly the countercultural movement of the sixties which, having now become part of recent history, appears to have indicated the existence of some affinity between Marxism and religious movements of an ideologically very different kind.

With the rapid growth of modern industrial capitalism in Europe there had emerged by the middle decades of the nineteenth century, especially in England where workers had been crammed into the high-density urban squalour of cities such as Manchester and Birmingham, a stark brutalisation of life in factories and slums, in the interests of Mammon; this was linked with a refusal by most of the middle class to admit that it was so,[1] or that the fault was any other than that of the poor themselves. On the other hand a few radical voices, those of artists, poets, journalists and intellectuals, Blake, Dickens, Dumas, Marx and others, were raised in protest against the dehumanisation of life which industrial capitalism entailed.

Associated with rapid development in the technologically based society during the middle decades of the twentieth century there has been a similar deep sense of human *malaise* and a protest against it. This, occurring at a time when trends, fashions and ideas were capable of being communicated over long distances by the public media and by the organs of popular culture, resulted in the growth and spread of new experiments and theories in alternative styles of life, and an increased adherence to radical attitudes towards the conventions of capitalist society. In Britain the countercultural movement was influenced by similar movements in the United States and the continent of Europe, which, in most of their phases, preceded that of Britain by a year or two.

(i) *Counterculture and ideology*

The countercultural movement of the 1960s had the effect of bringing into close juxtaposition for a while what appeared to be two contrasting views of life. One is Marxist in various forms and the other is religious, especially mystical, also in various forms. The counterculture of the sixties, with its own special characteristics, is now receding into the past, but it still has a certain resonance and is worth examining in retrospect. Such an undertaking will have a more than retrospective interest however, for counterculture, in some form or another, appears to be a continuing mood or emphasis in Western industrial society. So long as the culture associated with such society, and in particular the official religious ideology which has stamped its character upon that culture, manages to continue in existence, the protest to which it gives rise appears likely to continue to find expression in these two characteristic forms, broadly Marxist and mystical.

There was an initial stage when the ferment of the sixties was seen as 'a cohesive and coherent whole within which no issue can be separated from the others'. Jean-François Revel listed ten such issues: a new approach to moral values; the black revolt; women's liberation; rejection of economic and social goals; advocacy of non-coercion in education; poverty; social equality; rejection of authoritarian culture; rejection of American power politics; and concern with the natural environment. These issues gained strength from one another; opposition to the Vietnam war was linked with male domination; rejection of parental economic social goals was linked with concern with poverty, racism, and concern for the environment, and so on. Revel went so far as to say: 'The moral revolution, the cultural revolution, and the political revolution are but a single revolution.'[2] He characterised the whole of this as 'a counter-culture'.

More sensitive to the finer distinctions is Stuart Halls' analysis[3] which takes serious account of 'the themes of mysticism and contemplation'.[4] These are seen as overlapping with hippie culture but not as identical with it. Just as the hippie scene expresses 'a new kind of togetherness' so too the Eastern philosophies have at their centre 'the notion of an all-embracing unity which underlies the varied multiplicity of life, the resolution of the Many in One'.[5] It is not a very extensive over-lap. Moreover Hall makes an important distinction between hippy and meditational movements. For the hippy there is only one way to experience the hidden utopia within the self and that is 'through the medium of mind-expanding drugs. Others (that is, meditators), by long discipline and the practice of asceticism, have managed to enter these forbidden realms of feeling. . . . But Hippies are in too much of a hurry, and disciplined asceticism too alien' for them to waste time on the long practice of meditation when a short trip via LSD is available.[6]

Other characteristics of hippy culture as Hall described it would seem to distinguish it from radical political movements also. For example, he drew attention to its extreme individualism. In part, he wrote, 'it springs from an assertion of the primacy of the imperatives of self as against the claims of society.' But beyond this it was 'rooted in the same soil as the American Constitution and the manifold myths of the free-enterprise, every-man-his-own President society'.[7]

Five years later Salter reported what he found to be a significant confirmation of the merger that had by then begun to take place between hippies and radical political protest. This had already been greeted in the USA by the *Weatherman*: 'Guns and grass are united in the youth underground. Freaks are revolutionaries and revolutionaries are freaks.'[8] Salter's study of students at Enfield College of Technology suggested similar conclusions: anti-System militancy, and anti-System hippy counterculture had begun to coalesce, possibly below university level in the schools.[9]

This left the specifically religious, or meditational type of counterculture more clearly defined, and now somewhat apart from hippy counterculture. For much of the period of the sixties hippy life had been a kind of temporary froth on the surface of the ferment, making differentiation between religious and radical political counterculture difficult, even if also to some extent providing a common ground or means of cultural transition between the two.

Contemporary counterculture in the West could possibly be seen as having a single 'push' (modern industrialism) and a number of distinguishable 'pull' factors. This might suggest that the former is primary: that it is the repulsion *from* one's culture which determines the actual coming into existence of a counterculture; and that without this the attraction of the various cultural alternatives would not be strongly felt, and that they might never become anything more than matters of casual interest. The term counterculture is used to describe a situation where (negatively) there is resistance, even if only on the part of a minority, to the values and norms of the dominant culture, and also where (positively) many of the values held by this minority 'are specifically contradictions of the values of dominant culture'.[10]

This raises the question of how the minority come to possess values which are contradictory to those of their own culture. How is it that only *some* people and not all are in revolt against the culture of modern industrialised society? Is it primarily because they have perceived from their actual experience or knowledge of another culture (a knowledge others do not have) that there are alternative values? A second positive explanation is that the culture of modern industrialised society itself engenders the spirit of revolt against itself, provoking it, so to speak, from within the human psyche without any outside aid, but only in the more sensitive individuals and among those who are able to revolt; what is sought as an alternative has then to be given a local habitation and a name, and is projected on to some distant, little known, romantically perceived culture such as that of India. Thus the idea, propagated by a certain kind of philosophical Indian writer, that the East is spiritual and mystical (in contrast to the West, which is materialistic and secular) gains credence among the cultural rebels of the West, and certain elements of Indian culture are thenceforth sought out and adopted as part of the new emerging or alternative culture.

If the main force of the countercultural 'push' is to be found in the rejection of the excessive materialism of capitalist society, then the cultural migrant who moves into some form of Marxist culture will find his rejection of contemporary culture is endorsed in his new environment. The question which arises in this connection is whether the migrant into some form of Hindu culture will find the same sort of endorsement there. Superficially from one example which has been highlighted in the literature it might seem that he will not, and will instead find himself back with the capitalist cultural ethic.

(ii) *The Krishna Consciousness movement*

The example referred to is one of the (allegedly) imported forms of Indian religion known in the West as the Hare Krishna movement, or ISKON (the International Society for Krishna Consciousness). The Society's publicity and propaganda, including expensively produced literature, and the dancing and singing of its shaven-headed devotees in the streets of the capitals and big cities of the West have, with the aid of the public media, made the movement familiar to American and European city dwellers at least. This exotic and uninhibited self-display is taken by Western spectators, understandably, to be a representative sample of Indian religion. They might be surprised to learn that in West Bengal, where the movement had its roots, it is regarded publicly with the same kind of tolerant amusement as in the West, with an additional relish provided by the fact that young Americans should be caught up in religious activity of this kind. From time to time English language newspapers in Bengal publish mildly patronising accounts of the latest developments in what is a mainly American-supported enterprise.

The movement was founded in the USA in 1966 by a Bengali, whose religious name is Bhaktivedanta Swami Prabhupada, who went to America specifically for that purpose in order to exercise his 'mission to the counterculture'.[11] In Bengal the roots of the movement are in one of the many Vaishnava salvation sects; but this particular sect has a fairly limited local popularity in West Bengal. So limited is its appeal among Bengalis that, as Judah records, 'in recent years hundreds of American devotees of Krishna have been sent to India as missionaries to the Indians. There they have been trying to revive and spread the message of Krishna Consciousness among the Hindu population.' He notes that they have had no great success: 'Garga Muri and others estimate that they have not converted more than twenty-five or thirty Hindus to their ranks.'[12] And that is in a part of Bengal where an area of about thirty miles by fifty miles (Nadia District) has a population of over $2\frac{1}{4}$ million.[13] The American devotees, whose efforts include the building of a very large multi-million dollar temple, feel that they have a mission to preserve Hindu culture which they see as being threatened by the widespread secularisation of life in India.

It is worth noting that one searches in vain in Bengal, the vanguard area of so many social and cultural movements in the past, for anything corresponding to the countercultural movement in the West. As elsewhere in India, the youth of the metropolitan area of Calcutta and the industrial towns of the Hooghly valley are interested primarily in getting enough money to enjoy the material possessions which Western countercultural youth disdains. The present writer spent several weeks in the spring of 1975 interviewing social scientists in Calcutta, with a view to finding evidence of any comparable countercultural movement in Bengal, but with no success.

The attitude of those Western young people who enter the Krishna Consciousness movement has been described as a rejection of the following aspects of Western industrialised society: (1) the quest for individual material success through competitive labour; (2) the kind of education which has that end in view; (3) acquisitiveness in terms of material possessions; (4) the kind of authority, parental and governmental, which favours the *status quo*; (5) any war, such as that in Vietnam, which is the outcome of imperialistic purpose with an economic basis; and (6) the hypocrisy of members of the Establishment with regard to civil rights and race relations.[14]

Most if not all these aspects of modern industrialised society rejected by those who have entered the Krishna Consciousness movement would be rejected also by other entrants into the counterculture, including (it is important to notice) those whose direction is generally more radical-political. If these are agreed in common opposition to such characteristic features of capitalist culture, it is a matter of some interest to find out whether traditional Hindu culture shares in this common opposition. It is with that question, and the variant forms of it in respect of other world religions, that this study is principally concerned.

The social background of those who enter the Krishna Consciousness movement is predominantly what Judah describes as 'upper middle class'. He reports that 'about 70 per cent of the parents of the Krishna devotees are members of one of the established churches or synagogues'. In detail, the affiliations of parents were: 18 per cent Roman Catholics; 29 per cent Protestant (Methodist, Episcopal, Presbyterian and Congregational), 14.5 per cent Jewish; and 12.5 per cent Mormon, Jehovah's Witnesses, and other sects. Only 25 per cent of the parents did not belong to an organised church or sect. Of the devotees whose parents were members of religious organisations, 81 per cent had received training in the faith of their parents. It is partly against the theologically liberal climate of the established American churches that the Krishna devotees appear to be reacting. They exhibit an intensely dogmatic and exclusivist spirit. They see the doctrines of their movement as the entire and only truth, and regard the infallible source of these doctrines as the scriptures of Gaudiya Vaisnavism literally interpreted. They regard the aim of the movement as entirely directed towards individuals; they are not interested in social problems, and regard social activism as doomed to failure because it does not get to the root of the human problem which is, how to bring individuals to Krishna Consciousness.[15] Judah points out that in these respects the movement closely resembles other countercultural religious groups in the USA and Britain such as the Jesus People, the Children of God, and the underground churches. Clearly at this point they have parted company with the radically political sector of the counter culture.

What is significant and interesting is the extent of the *Hindu* effect; Judah sees certain parallels between the Puritan ethic of the early Calvinist and that of the Krishna devotee. The latter develops a sense of being totally surrendered to God (Krishna) and accepts the doctrine of the total sovereignty of God over man. Krishna alone controls the grace by which man is saved. The use of material goods for one's own sense of gratification is firmly forbidden. Materialistic desires of any kind are discouraged. Restrictions on sexual activity are very strict. Marriage is for life and widows are not allowed to remarry (even those who have been 'widowed' by their husbands becoming full-time ascetics), and within marriage sexual intercourse is allowed solely for the purpose of procreating.[16] This might appear to indicate that Hindu culture is a favourable environment for the emergence of entrepreneurship.

The Krishna devotee does not seem to have the same compulsion to work, however, as the Calvinist. This is perhaps due to the conscious strength of his revolt against the work ethic of the American Establishment, and because he has rejected the idea of strenuous productive labour which, in his view, merely goes to support the American government and American society. A case of this sort is mentioned by Judah. the man concerned was prepared to work at a job in the Society's incense factory, however, because the environment was congenial, the company was pleasant, and he had the knowledge that he was working for God.[17] But compared with the early Calvinist the Krishna devotee appears to have a somewhat ambivalent attitude to productive labour.

(iii) *The end of an age*   ·

One common feature to be found among all the elements in the counterculture is the idea of the approaching end of an age. This is a theme found not only among Marxists but also among those elements of the counterculture which are primarily concerned with the occult and the esoteric. Judah quotes two exchanges of conversation overheard on the campus at San Francisco in December 1973: 'I understand the Aquarian Age will actually begin in 1980.' And between two other people next day: 'I agree with you entirely that the myth of Christmas ended in the sixties.'[18]

The same theme is found in Tiryakian's *The Margin of the Visible* (1974). This is a collection of pieces by various writers, some written recently, and some earlier, as, for instance, those by P. D. Ouspensky, Carl Jung, Geog Simmel and others. About thirty separate pieces are included, all of which in some way help to illustrate Tiryakian's central theme, namely, that a key component of the dynamism of Western civilisation, the 'theurgic restlessness' at the heart of the Western historical process, is in part a function of the marginal status of esoteric subculture as an active 'counterculture' which has been a seed-bed of innovations and inspirations in religion, science, politics and other domains such as art and literature. Tiryakian's interpretation of how theurgic restlessness shows itself is that in crucial periods of *anomie* (in the Durkheimian sense) esoteric and occult doctrines and practices come to the surface from their normally covert level and attain public visibility or, in other words, appear in the form of counterculture. The flourishing of the esoteric and the occult have, therefore, 'a definite sociological significance'. It might, observes Tiryakian, be an indicator of advanced cultural decadence: 'It is also conceivable that it may be a harbinger of a new cultural paradigm.' This upsurge of interest in the occult and the esoteric which has occurred recently, and which can be regarded as a distinct and separate aspect of the counterculture, is remarkable in that it has come in a period such as the present which in many ways represents an advanced state of modernity. This does not mean that the phenomenon has to be interpreted as a 'breakdown of modernization' (*pace* Eisenstadt), a flight into the irrational in order to escape from the strains of a technological society. 'To posit that a flourish of the occult represents a "breakdown of modernization" is not an explanation of why it should occur at this time,' nor an explanation of its meaning to various social strata, comments Tiryakian. An adequate sociological explanation would make it possible to interpret, more positively than the 'breakdown' theory does, those other occasions in Western civilisation when 'renewal of interest and participation in the esoteric and the occult took place, notably during the Renaissance and Reformation and during the closing stages of the Roman Empire'.[19] Tiryakian concludes that the present revival of the occult and the esoteric is comparable with such previous occasions. The core of the problem of interpretation here, he considers, is in striking a viable balance between two dimensions which he calls broadly 'subjectivity' and 'objectivity' with regard to man's understanding of the world. This is a problem at the heart of the direction of modern society and therefore, he claims, 'a crucial sociological problem'.

Concern with the balance between a proper human subjectivity and objectivity, in this sense, underlies the thought of Karl Marx also. Further, if this is 'a crucial sociological problem' it may well have a close connection with what Michael Hill and Donald MacRae have both called the 'central concern of sociological theory', namely religion understood in a broad sense.[20] It is significant that for Marx also 'the criticism of religion is the premise of all criticism'.[21]

Certainly religion held a fairly central place in the thought and writing of the man who is credited with the first use of the word 'sociology', namely August Comte (1789–1867). Comte was, in principle, concerned with an issue which nearly a century and a half later characterised the counterculture of the 1960s, namely, a sense of the social and intellectual transformation which is demanded of those who have to live henceforth in an industrial society.

The view of the human situation as one in which one age is dying and a new about to begin is common in sociology. It has been so from the time of Comte until now. Because the old order of things is passing away with the emergence of modern industrial society it is of prime importance, argued Comte, to engage in serious scientific study of the nature of society as it actually exists, and in the light of such a science to draw out the lineaments of the new social system which must take its place. Two movements, wrote Comte, 'agitate society; one a movement of disorganisation, the other of reorganisation. By the former, considered apart, society is hurried towards a profound moral and political anarchy which appears to menace it with a near and inevitable dissolution. By the latter it is guided to the definitive social condition of the human race, that best suited to its nature, in which all progressive movements should receive their completest development and more direct application. In the coexistence of these two opposed tendencies consists the grand crisis now experienced by the most civilised nations; and this can only be understood when viewed under both aspects.

> From the moment when this crisis began to show itself down to the present time the tendency of the ancient system to disorganisation has predominated, or rather, this alone is all that is *plainly* manifested. It was in the nature of things that the crisis should begin thus, so that the old system might be sufficiently modified to permit the direct formation of the new social system.

These words of Comte are from his essay, first published in May 1882, entitled 'Plan for the Scientific Operations Necessary for Reorganising Society'.[22]

The difficulties of the modern situation, according to Comte, are due to the fact that 'until the new system has been inaugurated, the preponderance still maintained by the negative tendency constitutes the

greatest obstacle to the progress of civilisation'.[23] One of the principal tasks
of sociology, therefore, is to explore this situation.

One reason why Comte's work is not widely studied is perhaps simply
that certain features of his programme have passed into the general
programme of sociology, and his principles have now received
elaboration in the work of later sociologists. But another important reason
is that although he wrestled energetically with the vast problems for
human thought which were presented by the industrial revolution, an
analysis of the nature of the crisis in industrial society was much more fully
developed by Karl Marx, his younger contemporary.

Comte did not repudiate industrial society as his older contemporary
William Blake (1757–1827) had done. However, Blake's is also a
countercultural voice in the sense of being a protest against a dominant,
lingering, and now oppressive ideology. He cries out against Newton's
mechanical astronomy and Locke's mechanical society:

> I turn my eyes to the Schools and Universities of Europe
> And there behold the Loom of Locke, whose woof wages dire,
> Washed by the Water-wheels of Newton: black the cloth
> In heavy wreathes folds over every Nation: cruel Works
> Of many Wheels I view, wheel within wheel, with cogs tyrannic
> Moving by compulsion each other, not as those in Eden, which,
> Wheel within wheel, in freedom revolve in harmony and peace.[24]

Blake's long poem 'Jerusalem', from which these lines are taken, is
resonant not only with the sounds of the Black Country ('Bromion's iron
Tongs and glowing Poker reddening fierce') but also with the lifeless
theology of the Church of England, and 'Abstract Philosophy warring in
enmity against Imagination'.[25] Blake was, as Bronowski has pointed out, a
man with a deep distaste for the Church of England and its ritual, a
dissenter the roots of whose dissent ran back to the Puritan Revolution
when the Divine Right of Kings was challenged, the King beheaded, and a
new society set up.[26]

The industrial revolution, which has profoundly changed and is
changing man's conception and understanding of himself, is barely 200
years old; its implications for human thought about the nature of the
universe man inhabits are still only beginning to be appreciated. Often the
industrial revolution is still regarded as an episode, merely marked for a
time by the emergence of wretchedly congested industrial slums and
brutish conditions in which working people were at that time forced to

live. Blake's experience was of that early kind of culture-shock; his were the pangs of revulsion at what was coming into being with the industrial age, pangs which were beginning to be felt everywhere. In this, as in other matters of a more directly political nature, Blake spoke, so he believed, for many of his time. He thought of himself as 'an honest man', uttering his opinion of public matters. He shared the common view.[27]

The countercultural movement of a century and a half later feeds on his early experience; and his words have a continuing resonance for many in a period when, as they see it, provision is being made for the internal combustion engine to stifle whatever kind of life is left to men living in increasing numbers in dependence on tranquillisers and anti-depressant drugs; to name only one of the apprehensions about the future which the counterculture expresses.

(iv) *Roszak and rationalism*

Theodore Roszak is one of the best known exponents of the protest against all this. His view of the counterculture,[28] well known enough to need no more than a mention here, ranges from Alan Watts to Marcuse, from Ginsberg to William Blake. Roszak's own preference, it seems, is for William Blake. In the same tradition Roszak pours out torrents of finely turned phrase in bitter criticism of industrial society. In *Where the Wasteland Ends*[29] he brings together much that is widely diffused common knowledge into a synoptic indictment of the industrialised nations and their relationship with the rest of the world.

Nevertheless his remedy for the modern condition, his 'visionary commonwealth' comes as an anticlimax. When the crucial issue, that of relating an analysis of the ills of industrial society to the social realities of the contemporary world, is reached, Roszak in effect shrugs off this whole project and retreats into an isolated individualism; at best he sees the solution in the resort to 'communitarian minorities' living on the fringes of the existing society in what is likely to be muted or ineffective protest. The groups he describes cannot be completely independent. Even if, for example, *sometimes* they do manage to provide from natural resources the means of lighting and heating their huts, this hardly provides a viable example for the majority of the population to follow. And no hint is given of any other programme of change. The important question, of how to get from the situation where a minority can live such simple lives on the fringe, a refined privileged élite, perhaps making selective use of the products of industrial society such as medicines and surgery, to where everyone can join in without all having to revert to the life of cave and forest, is not answered. The problem is too politically and economically complex to be dealt with satisfactorily at the level of dilettante romanticism.

Roszak, however, is not concerned to present a rational argument. Understandably 'rational' is for him a pejorative word. His writing confirms this: it is impressionistic, inspirational, and in this and other respects highly redolent of the preaching of Billy Graham which he mentions with disdain for its mere theatricality. While he does acknowledge, on the last page of *Where the Wasteland Ends*, that there *is* an incompleteness in the historical process, he elsewhere asserts again and again that 'Gnosis needs no history.' Gnosis is the experience of Romantics who 'saw a timeless self-fulfilment'. He insists that complete and perfect vision of the 'truth' is possible here and now. 'You can see it all – eternity reflected in the mirror of time, you *can*!' he proclaims. Like all gnostics Roszak does not accept that there may still be an incompleteness in our knowledge, our understanding, our vision, which we have no option but to accept. This is intolerable and therefore is denied. Yet perhaps ultimately an *a-gnostic* attitude is more deeply convincing and satisfying – to have before us the prospect that there is always more yet to be understood, and that the human condition is one which demands scientific openness to new evidence and new knowledge.

Roszak sees the origin of the counterculture of the sixties, in general terms, simply in terms of the excessive *industrialism* of Western society. Norman Birnbaum regards this as a misreading of the situation. He considers Roszak is mistaken in his interpretation of the counterculture as a revolt against industrialism; it is, in Birnbaum's view, only a revolt against certain facets of *American* life, such as racial oppression, the educational bureaucracies, imperialist wars, and its assault on nature.[30] Now if this were so one would suppose that industrialism of a different kind – say a Russian Communist kind – might be free from such youthful rejection, and not embarrassed by the search for cultural alternatives to what the Establishment offers.

(v) *Soviet youth and the sects*

A recent study by Christel Lane suggests this is not the case.[31] A problem for Soviet sociologists, more serious than that of the persistence of the Russian Orthodox Church, is the growth of religious sects, both indigenous and of Western origin. The indigenous Russian sects, whose existence dates back to before the revolution, have declined, but less so than the Russian Orthodox Church, and, what is more significant, the members of the sects are generally less elderly and less nominal in their adherence than are the majority of the Orthodox. The most persistent and active sects are those of Western origin – Baptists, Pentecostalists, Jehovah's Witnesses, Menonites and Adventists. Lane reports that Soviet writers 'show particular concern over the fact that in the sixties [the sects] have attracted an increasing proportion of young, urban, well-educated and well-qualified people who have had the full benefit of Soviet social provisions and political education'.[32]

Among the more cogent explanations offered by Soviet sociologists is one which emphasises that religiosity has roots which are partly ideological and partly psychological, and that it is the latter which have been largely responsible for this trend among a minority of the younger generation. Certain psychological needs are felt in certain sections of society, needs for which church attendance can provide satisfaction. It does so 'because they relish the emotional impact of ritual and because the beauty and solemnity of the church satisfies their aesthetic requirements and their longing for calmness and peace'.[33] Another explanation is that church attendance is resorted to as a way of dealing with strongly felt personal difficulties – failure, illness, death, loneliness, broken re-lationships, and so on. To a Marxist theoretician the fact that such needs are strongly felt and have to be satisfied by recourse to 'religion' seems to indicate that Soviet society has not yet been made fully socialist and ultimately, therefore, this explanation is an admission of inadequate social reconstruction. But the areas which Soviet sociologists have acknowled-ged are incompletely reconstructed, and where full socialism has not been reached, are other than the areas where this kind of religious adherence is found; the areas hitherto identified as 'backward' were rural, socially isolated areas with a predominance of low-skilled occupations and elderly people. The strength of the sects, however, is found among some of the urban, socialised young. Lane points out that the psychological type of explanation 'implies the completely non-Marxist hypothesis that religion is a universal phenomenon existing in any society regardless of its social system'.[34]

Lane's own explanation of the persistence of the sects' power to attract is that membership of a sect 'serves as a vehicle for expressing ideological protest' in a situation where Soviet communist ideology has failed to meet the ethical needs of relatively unsophisticated, recently urbanised groups;

they experience it as oppressive, but as they have no avenues open to them for political expression of their dissatisfaction, they express it, she says, by identifying with the only non-communist ideology available to them, that of the Christian sects.

Another possibility is that since these are recently urbanised groups, and since Soviet industrial society increasingly resembles all other forms of modern industrial culture in its mechanical, anti-personal quality and its remoteness from the natural world, there may be seen to be here an experience among these young people which is similar in many of its characteristic features to that of the young in other industrialised, Western countries. Both forms of counterculture, the American and the Soviet, appear to be the consequence of psychological and ideological factors. These factors have their origins in American industrial society and in Soviet industrial society. But the common element is not simply industrialism, *per se*. The fact that there is a strong *ideological* element in the countercultural protest indicates also dissatisfaction with the dominant ideology which has failed to meet the moral and aesthetic needs of some of the rising generation. One might almost say that it refers to 'an expression of real suffering and a protest against real suffering . . . the sigh of the oppressed creature, the sentiment of a heartless world, and the soul of soulless conditions . . . the opium of the people'. When Karl Marx wrote these words in 1843 he was characterising the role of Christian religion as he believed it to be at that time. But adherence to Christianity in the industrialising societies of that period was confined very largely to the bourgeoisie. The bishop of London commented on the almost unchurched condition of the working classes in England at the end of the nineteenth century, to the effect that it was not that the Church had lost them: it had never had them.

One difficulty with Marx's critique of religion is that in predominantly Protestant countries at least, organised religion in the nineteenth and early twentieth centuries was located primarily among the middle classes; even that relatively small proportion which Methodism ushered in to the Church soon became middle-class, either in reality or in outlook, as John Wesley himself noted.[35] Similarly in mid-twentieth century, protest against the inadequacies of the dominant culture in those countries was again located primarily in the middle classes. The majority of the working class was not interested in the question, one way or the other. The counterculture which has shown itself among educated, urban Soviet youth has a basis which it shares with American and western-European counterculture. The dominant ideology against which they all are united in protest is that of bureaucratic capitalism. The Soviet system of state capitalism appears to have effects on some of the new generation of young Soviet adults similar to those which the capitalism of the gigantic American corporations has had upon young Americans. More precisely the various forms of counterculture in the West can be seen as protests against the *dehumanising materialism of modern capitalist society*. Against this complex of ideal and material factors the various separate emphases and forms within the counterculture have each protested selectively, according to their scale of priorities. Whereas all have started from a basic feeling of dissatisfaction and even alienation, some have identified the *materialism* of contemporary society as the root of the trouble and have sought a remedy in spiritual, mystical and meditational cults, while others, recognising the degree to which human life is conditioned by economic factors, have identified the *dehumanising* effect of *capitalism* as the cause and have sought a remedy in Marxist humanism. The latter course has good antecedents. Among critiques of Soviet society and ideology there has been no lack of those which have proceeded from Marxist premises such as those of Plamenatz[36] and Marcuse[37], etc.

The perception by both Marxists and hippies in the countercultural movement of the sixties, that they had a common interest, was not altogether mistaken. They can be seen in broad terms to have shared with William Blake and Karl Marx a rejection of the dehumanising aspects of a system in which financial profitability is the ultimate criterion, and which overrides every other kind of consideration.

As Anthony Giddens has pointed out, 'the critical assessment of the characteristic mode of life stimulated in capitalism is quite remarkably similar in the writings of both [Marx and Weber].' Both writers regard mature capitalism 'as a world in which religion is replaced by a social organisation in which technological rationality reigns supreme'.[38] In Weber's view it was specifically the bureaucratic routine, fostered by capitalism, which was associated with the dehumanising of life. Developed bureaucracy, 'which is welcomed by capitalism, develops the more completely, the more the bureaucracy is "dehumanised", the more completely it succeeds in eliminating from official business, love, hatred, and all personal, irrational and emotional elements which escape calculation'.[39]

Countercultural movements understandably, therefore, have in general attempted to reverse the dehumanising trend of bureaucratic rationality; in order to restore those attitudes and agencies which enhance human personal relationships and deepen self-understanding.

Positive opposition to the dominant culture, especially where that culture has a strongly, although conventionally, religious element which is closely associated with the governmental system, is in certain circumstances implicitly an attitude subversive of the existing order. This raises the question whether the state in which the dominant culture is of a Soviet Communist kind is also to be regarded in the same way; or, to put it in other words, whether Soviet Communist ideology has the same function as a dominant conventional religion in a bourgeois state, that of providing popular support for the *status quo* through a kind of mystification which projects an illusory unity where none exists.

NOTES

1. See F. Engels, *The Condition of the Working Class in England* (English edn, 1973), p. 57.

2. J. F. Revel, *Without Marx or Jesus* (1972), p. 168.

3. Stuart Hall's 'The Hippies and Dissent in America', in *Problems of Modern Society*, ed. P. Worsley (1972).

4. Hall, p. 597.

5. Ibid., p. 598.

6. Ibid., p. 601.

7. Ibid., p. 601f.

8. D. Horowitz, *et al.* (eds), *Counterculture and Revolution* (1972), xi.

9. B. G. Salter, 'Student Militants and Counterculture', in *Universities Quarterly* (Autumn 1974), p. 467.

10. J. M. Yinger, 'Contraculture and Subculture', in *American Sociological Review*, vol. 25, no. 5 (1960), p. 629.

11. J. S. Judah, *Hare Krishna and the Counterculture* (1974), p. 16.

12. Ibid., p. 43.

13. *1971 Census of India*, Series 22, West Bengal, Pt IIA (1973), p. 20.

14. Judah, p. 16.

15. Ibid., p. 145f.

16. Ibid., p. 124f.

17. Ibid., p. 175f.

18. Ibid., p. 197.

19. A. E. Tiryakian, *The Margin of the Visible* (1974), p. 2.

20. Michael Hill, *A Sociology of Religion* (1973), p. viii and p. 266.

21. *MECW*, vol. 3, p. 175.

22. R. Fletcher, *The Crisis of Industrial Civilisation: The Early Essays of A. Comte* (1974), p. 111.

23. Ibid.

24. W. Blake, *Jerusalem* Plate 15, lines 14ff. See G. Keynes, *Blake's Complete Writings* (1966), p. 636.

25. Keynes, p. 624.

26. J. Bronowski, *William Blake and the Age of Revolution* (1972), p. 11f.

27. D. V. Erdman, *Blake, Prophet Against Empire* (1954), pp. iii and 5.

28. T. Roszak, *The Making of a Counterculture* (1969).

29. —————— *Where the Wasteland Ends* (1972), pp. 435ff, 442f and 448.

30. N. Birnbaum, *Towards a Critical Sociology* (1971), p. 366.

31. C. Lane, 'Some explanations for the persistence of Christian religion in Soviet society', in *Sociology*, vol. 8, no. 2 (May 1974).

32. Ibid., p. 235.

33. Ibid., p. 238.

34. Ibid.

35. See M. Weber, *The Protestant Ethic and the Spirit of Capitalism* (1930, repr. 1976), p. 175.

36. J. Plamenatz, *German Marxism and Russian Communism* (1954).

37. Herbert Marcuse, *Soviet Marxism: A Critical Analysis* (1958).

38. A. Giddens, *Capitalism and Modern Social Theory* (1971), p. 215.

39. Max Weber, *Economy and Society*, 3 vols (1968), p. 975.

10 Marxism as Religion?

(i) *The chorus of assent*

SOME people have no doubts about the proposition, 'Marxism is a religion.' It could be argued that the bulk of literature supporting the view that Marxism is a religion is so great that it cannot easily be set aside. On the other hand there is the fact that this literature is written almost exclusively by non-Marxists. Marxists differ in their view of the primary nature of Marxism, but along quite other lines than these. Some see it as primarily a philosophical system, others as an economic analysis and programme, while yet others regard it as primarily concerned with political action. This third view is held, for example, by Robin Blackburn:

> The real originality of Marx and Engels lies in the field of politics, not in economics or philosophy. . . . Unfortunately, there has been an increasing tendency in twentieth-century Marxism to identify the philosophical method of epistemology employed by Marx or Engels as their crucial contribution, and to represent these as the touchstones of Marxist orthodoxy. In different ways this is done by the Lukács of *History and Class Consciousness*, the exponents of Soviet Diamat and Louis Althusser and his collaborators in *Reading Capital*. There is little equivalent insistence on the originality of the political conceptions of Marx and Engels. . . . Moreover, it is evident that all the major divisions of Marxism have arisen over directly political questions, which have thereby furnished the critical determinants of Marxist 'orthodoxy'. This does not mean that philosophical or epistemological disputes have had no significance for Marxism. It does mean that they have emerged as secondary by-products of conflicts over substantive political questions.[1]

At what point, then, can the allegedly 'religious' character emerge, in view of the fact that this kind of summary of the possible ways of understanding Marxism appears to exclude altogether any religious character? At the beginning of this book it was pointed out that there are various distinguishable forms of Marxism; the question has, therefore, to be given a more specific form: Is *any* one of the varieties of Marxism to be regarded as a religion or a proto-religion, and if so on what grounds?

Certainly the roots of Marxism appear to lie in the realm of religion. It would not be surprising to find strands of thought in Marxism which are of specific religious origin. There is, in the first place, Karl Marx's own Jewish heritage, his rabbinical ancestry, and his own conscious reaction against the Lutheran religion which his father had been forced to adopt. Reaction against one form of religion does not necessarily constitute irreligion. Karl Marx showed a certain intellectual interest in religious problems in his school days. The doctrines of Saint-Simon, which strongly influenced him in his youth, were recognised in the Germany of his day as religious in nature. In the Moselle region, where these doctrines were gaining many adherents, 'the archbishop was obliged to issue a special warning against *this new heresy*'.[2]

One of Lenin's recent biographers writes of early associates of Lenin as 'men whose whole lives had been bound up with the bracing appeal of Marxism, for whom it was not only a political creed but a religion and a way of life'. There is here, he comments, a 'stern moral judgment and doom pronounced upon the rich and powerful of this world, all the more satisfying, for it cannot be avoided or softened'.[3] This immediately recalls the prophetic activity of Muhammad's days in Mecca; every word applies exactly to the message of early Islam to the rich men of Mecca. 'It is no wonder that for all its materialistic and free-thinking base Marxism has always held a secret attraction for some religious-minded; it promises, and considerably sooner than in the next world, certain chastisement for those who have succumbed to the false idols of worldly success.'[4]

Similarly Karl Popper, in the course of his long critical study of Marx, having characterised Marxism as 'moral theory' and 'oracular philosophy', declares that he would 'be the last to deny its religious character'.[5] The American economist J. E. Schumpeter affirms categorically: 'Marxism *is* a religion. To the believer it presents, first, a system of ultimate ends that embody the meaning of life and are absolute standards by which to judge events and actions; and secondly a guide to those ends which implies a plan of salvation and the indication of the evil from which mankind, or a chosen section of mankind, is to be saved.'[6]

(ii) *A meaningless proposition*

The statement 'Marxism is a religion' is, however, vacuous. One undefined term is being equated with another. If any attempt is to be made to clarify the issue, the question *'which* Marxism?' must be considered, and then the question of how the word 'religion' is being used. The notorious ambiguity of this word has to be recognised and allowed for. For the same phenomena which in some people's view constitute 'religion' in other people's view do not. The reader is invited, therefore, to consider the following case. It is that of a movement which arose subsequent to the rise of Christianity, and was until recently regarded by the Christians of Europe as the arch-enemy of Christianity's claim to universal acceptance.

In its earliest days this movement took the form of radical opposition to the rich and powerful. Its founder pronounced moral judgements against them in the strongest terms and predicted their coming doom; those who had worshipped the false idols of money and privilege and had oppressed the poor would themselves be reviled and disinherited, on a day which he now saw coming over the horizon.

After an initial period of persecution and considerable struggle with the local authorities in the area in which the movement had arisen, it succeeded in spreading beyond these narrower borders into the wider world and a few years later achieved a notable success when a new state was set up which claimed to be based upon its principles. This became the centre from which the movement then spread even more rapidly to neighbouring countries, many of whose peoples were impressed by the success of the new doctrines.

As it spread it changed its character and eventually, when it reached its eastern limits, it assumed forms which were criticised, by its orthodox exponents in the land of its origin, as heretical. In becoming a world movement it had suffered diversification, in the same manner as had other world-movements. Quite early in its history it was found necessary to have recourse to the exact words of the founder in order to settle disputes; these words were, therefore, brought together into great collections and given definitive form and authoritative status.

It came to be regarded by the Christian Church as its principal ideological enemy, and the very name of the hated rival doctrine was enough to produce an instant reaction of moral indignation and dire warnings concerning the threat to Christendom which its existence posed.

Nevertheless it continued to gain converts, especially in those places where men had suffered too long from the elaborations and sophistry of the theologians and the incredibility of the doctrines these worthies produced. Those who wanted only a direct guide to action and a simple creed without complicating qualifications found them in this immensely appealing popular movement. Traditionally Christian areas of the world changed allegiance and became part of the new ideological empire which was being created.

But the new faith also made demands. It required of its devotees total unhesitating belief in its simple propositions, dedicated service, and absolute readiness to sacrifice themselves to the cause in violent action if necessary; such was in fact held to be the ultimate service which every true believer should be prepared to give sooner or later.

The question which must now be considered is whether the movement which has just been described qualifies in conventional terms as a 'religion'. There are, however, *two* movements which have arisen in the Christian era, both of which the foregoing description fits.

If in answer to the question 'Is this movement a religion?' the answer 'No' is given, then this entails the judgement that Islam is not a religion. For it is Islam which has been described. Nevertheless, to assert that Islam is not a religion is contrary to accepted usage. On the other hand, if the question receives the answer 'Yes' then it follows that classical German Marxism *is* a religion. For that, too, is the movement which has been described.

There is, however, one major point of difference between Islam and classical German Marxism which was omitted from the foregoing description and which anyone describing the principal characteristics of these two would be bound to mention, namely, that Islam gives a place of dominant importance to belief in a divine omnipotent creator, whereas classical Marxism has no place at all for such belief. Now if belief in a divine, omnipotent creator is the *sine qua non* of any system that is to be called religion, it follows that Marxism is not a religion. But it follows also from this that the system of thought and practice known as Theravada Buddhism, found in India, Sri Lanka and south-east Asia is not a religion, since it, too, has no doctrine of God. Some of its adherents would not dispute this conclusion, but in general Theravada Buddhism has been regarded as a religion in contexts where studies of religion are being undertaken, and systems of thought and philosophy are being classified. For although Theravada Buddhism is non-theistic, or agnostic about the idea of a creator-god, nevertheless its central affirmations include both the characterisation of empirical human existence as inherently unsatisfactory, and a *belief* in the possibility of it transcendence by means of the enlightenment gained by the Buddha. It is this which seems to give Theravada Buddhism the quality of a religion and which accounts for its general acceptance as such. This means that belief in a creator-god is not an indispensable qualification by which a movement passes, conventionally, as 'religious'. It is, rather, belief in some existence-transcending reality. Of *this* basic feature of 'religion', therefore, belief in a creator-god is one example among others. Implicit in the notion of an existence-transcending reality is the belief that through knowledge of this reality the present unsatisfactoriness of life is to be overcome.

(iii) *Marxism as belief*

If this is accepted, can classical Marxism once again be regarded in the same category as Islam, as a religion, even though it does not affirm the existence of an omnipotent divine creator and is severely critical of such a belief? May not Marxism qualify for inclusion on the ground that it is a form of belief in a reality that transcends empirical existence, and that by means of this reality, according to Marxist doctrine, the present unsatisfactoriness of the world is to be overcome? The answer depends on finding in Marxist thought some element which can fairly be represented as such a transcendent reality.

Attempts have been made to represent 'history' as having a place in classical Marxism equivalent to that which is held in theistic systems by God, or in Theravada Buddhism by enlightenment. History, it is said, has just this present-world-transcending quality; it is 'history' to which Marxism appeals as an ally, so to speak, and history which stands over and above mankind in some sublime providential role as 'a new metaphysical sovereign'. Kamenka, for example, speaks of the seizure of power by the Communist Party in Russia 'in the name of a new metaphysical sovereign: history itself'. This, he says, was the outcome of Marx's 'proclamation of an ultimate goal supported by history'.[7]

Others have seen a religious signification in the insistence of Marx upon the complementary nature of theory *and* practice. 'The philosophers have only interpreted the world in various ways; the point, however, is to change it.'[8] That is to say, thought and action are equally necessary; *praxis* is required in order to validate Marxist *theoria*, and the theory is only properly understood in the practice. This certainly is a feature which classical Marxism shares with Theravada Buddhism. However, the emphasis is laid equally on both theory and practice; the former is not to be ignored in the interests of the latter.

One recent critic, Robert Wesson, finds the 'religious' character of Marxism most clearly indicated in its 'metaphysics of revolution', a phrase used originally by George Lichtheim,[9] although he used it in connection with German Idealism. This hardly makes German Idealism a 'religion'. Nevertheless Wesson writes as follows:

> Marxism is more revelation than theory, a surrogate faith for an age losing its religion. Marx had the self-assurance of a prophet who has talked with God, and his way of oversimplifying issues through convoluted argument befits a dogma. He was a poet, prophet and moralist speaking as a philosopher and economist; his doctrine is not to be tested against mere facts but to be received as ethical religious truth. His categories and concepts are not to be concretely defined but directly apprehended by the spirit. Marxists unlike Darwinians, claim orthodoxy as a virtue. Marx's hatred of traditional religions was bitter beyond the requirements of his theory (in Marx's view, not only was religion 'the opium of the people', but the priest was also the moral equivalent of the hangman in upholding class rule), and it suggests the hatred of the new dispensation for the old.[10]

This passage has been quoted at length because it illustrates the indiscriminating use of the word 'religion' which characterises a good deal of the discussion of Marxism, and also the simplistic attitude adopted in some studies of Marx's critique of religion. To speak of Marx's hatred of 'traditional religions' in the plural, without qualification, is to construct a universal statement on too narrow a basis. Moreover Marx's attitude to European Christianity is not so much one of hatred and bitterness as of firm conviction in the rightness of his analysis, and possibly some scorn. If the priest was regarded by him as the moral equivalent of the hangman, it was the priest of state-established religion in Europe whom Marx evidently had in mind. While Marx was capable of strong feelings of a kind which it would not be improper to describe as religious, he appears to have entertained an attitude of contempt towards conventional religion in Germany. This notwithstanding, Marx's concern for the socially and economically oppressed and his abandonment of the relatively comfortable bourgeois background of his childhood and youth in the interests of revolution appear to justify Wesson's characterisation of him as 'a poet, prophet and moralist speaking as a philosopher and economist'. The positive tone of Marx's references to Boehme and other mystics, which was noted in chapter 2, is in keeping with his own highly articulate, emotional and prophetic style.

Thus the crucial difference between Marx on the one hand and on the other the Protestantism he knew in Germany and criticised for its oppressive character, is not a difference simply between the 'new' and the 'old'; more precisely it is a difference between the radical, the prophet, possibly the humanist, and the kind of institutionalised and 'stately' religion that legitimises and upholds a government which has a vested interest in preserving conditions of social inequality, a government, moreover, which in the pursuit of this aim makes subtle and mystifying use of institutional religion. This, as we have seen, is the force of Marx's critique of the religious institutions in his own culture; beyond that, his critique of 'religion' is virtually non-existent, as we found in chapter 5.

(iv) *Marxism and Soviet state ideology*

Since Marx's lifetime his ideas have been taken up and used, and in the case of their use by the Russian state they have suffered the same fate as the teachings of various prophets in the course of history, namely, that of being exploited for purposes which are at variance with the ideas themselves. The precise opposite of the original teaching then came to be practised, albeit in the name of that teaching. Of the various ways in which the Soviet Union has stood Marxism on its head, the most obvious is its attitude to religious ideology. Recognition of this entails recognition of more than one 'Marxism'; the new type is, in Marcuse's description, 'Soviet Marxism'.

Marx's view was that the tenets of Christian theologians would in the modern world cease to have any continuing relevance and that they would survive only in those societies where capitalism maintained its hold, and where the artificial two-fold division of humanity into lords and masters on the one hand and servants on the other was perpetuated. The exception to this would be where the Church's influence was *fortified* by the State. In a society in which a socialist structure had been established, theistic ideas might be expected to decline naturally. In general no special attention would need to be given to the eradication of theistic belief; it could simply be disregarded. The quite *incorrect* course of action, as not only Marx but Lenin after him made clear, is to *persecute* those who continue to adhere to theistic beliefs.

The number of states which claim to give official expression to the religious beliefs of their citizens is fewer now than in Marx's day. Here and there the state-established church still holds a place of influence which is quite disproportionate to the degree of public support it receives from the majority of the citizens. In such states as in Britain, for example, religious leaders and opinion-formers insist that they know better than most people what is good for most people and appear to have no compunction about trying to impose their world-view, their mythology, their ideology and their morality on others. An effective way of doing this is to assert continually that most other people really do believe as they do, in spite of the apparent evidence to the contrary. Religious belief and practice in fact remain minimal, and Britain qualifies as 'the most secular nation in Europe', with the small minority of middle-class churchgoers (less than 5 per cent of the population attending the Easter Communion in the Church of England) becoming increasingly aware of the distance that separates them from the mainstream of national culture.[11] The situation entails the hypocrisy of a nation which is overwhelmingly non-Christian pretending on official occasions and in official contexts to be Christian.

Marx's attitude to religion then, so far as his writings can be used as evidence, was one of opposition to it in its 'mystifying' forms, that is, when it disguised the interests of an economically privileged class. With this went a recognition that the critique of *such* religion provided a convenient entry point for a critique of society in which economic privilege flourished; and beyond that Marx's attitude was mainly indifference. The Soviet Union's attitude to Christian religion within its borders has been more strident, possibly more nervous, and certainly more openly and strenuously hostile. This is essentially the nature of the hostility of one ideology for another. The parallel with Islam is again instructive.

It is not, however, from what it has inherited from classical German Marxism that the Soviet Union has forged its Communist ideology, fiercely hostile to other religious ideologies. The sources of the Soviet cult are more Russian than Marxist. A full explication of this would take us well outside the limits of the present study of the relation between Marx and religion, for it properly forms part of the study of Russian religious history. It may be noted, however, that a number of historians have identified what they see as a Russian messianism, a belief in the unique role in history of 'Holy Russia', and of Moscow as the Third Rome. Vatro Murvar, for instance, has written of the messianic characteristics of Bolshevism.[12] This has now, he says, using Weber's description of the later history of a prophetic movement, become 'institutionalised and routinised into a gigantic power structure', and adds that while 'religious messianism is still of considerable concern to the Soviet rulers, there are no more revolutionary messianic structures in the Soviet Union today able to compete with the successfully modified messianism of the Bolsheviks' [13]

The fact that Karl Marx vigorously criticised the conventional, organised religion of his own day could be taken as evidence that he was himself adopting a religious stance. There is a sense in which Marx was more religious than Weber in that he entertained strong feelings against religion while Weber, for all his intellectual commitment to the superiority of western-European Christian culture, was, as he himself put it, 'religiously tone deaf'. Marx's followers have sensed something of this quality in his ideas and attitudes and have themselves demonstrated as much in the fervour with which they have promoted the Marxist understanding of the human condition. The danger which has been present in many such cases before, and is present in this one also, is that before long the word of the prophet becomes the sacred text of the orthodox. The living force of his vision hardens into the ritual chanting of shibboleths, and in the end the conventional respect which comes to be afforded to the prophet's name is captured and canalised by the manipulators of political power, whether in the Mughal empire or the Anglican state, or in modern Buddhist Thailand or the Soviet Union. This appears to have been the course of events again and again in the history of religion. Perhaps Karl Marx provides the latest example of the prophet's fate.

NOTES

1. *New Left Review*, no. 97 (May–June 1976), p. 3f.

2. T. B. Bottomore and Maximilien Rubel, *Karl Marx; Selected Writings in Sociology and Social Philosophy* (1963), p. 25 (emphasis added).

3. Adam B. Ulam, *Lenin and the Bolsheviks* (Fontana edn, 1969), p. 182.

4. Ibid.

5. Karl Popper, *The Open Society and its Enemies*, vol. 2 (1962), p. 255.

6. J. E. Schumpeter, *Capitalism, Socialism and Democracy* (1950), p. 5.

7. Eugene Kamenka, *The Ethical Foundations of Marxism* (2nd edn, 1972), p. 198.

8. The eleventh of Marx's 'Theses on Feuerbach', in Engels's version, *MECW*, vol. 5, p. 8; compare *MECW*, vol. 5, p. 6.

9. George Lichtheim, *Marxism: An Historical and Critical Study* (2nd edn, revised, 1964), p. 24.

10. Robert G. Wesson, *Why Marxism?* (1976), p. 29.

11. *The Times* (London, 10 August 1976), p. 3.

12. Vatro Murvar, 'Messianism in Russia: Religious and Revolutionary', in *Journal for the Scientific Study of Religion*, 10, no. 4 (Winter 1971).

13. Ibid. p. 334.

Index